AFTER CRYSTAL NIGHT

A Play In Two Acts

by
John Herman Shaner

SAMUEL FRENCH, INC.
45 WEST 25TH STREET   NEW YORK 10010
7623 SUNSET BOULEVARD HOLLYWOOD 90046
LONDON   TORONTO

Copyright ©, 1986, by John Herman Shaner

ALL RIGHTS RESERVED

CAUTION: Professionals and amateurs are hereby warned that AFTER CRYSTAL NIGHT is subject to a royalty. It is fully protected under the copyright laws of the United States of America, the British Commonwealth, including Canada, and all other countries of the Copyright Union. All rights, including professional, amateur, motion pictures, recitation, lecturing, public reading, radio broadcasting, television, and the rights of translation into foreign languages are strictly reserved. In its present form the play is dedicated to the reading public only.

AFTER CRYSTAL NIGHT may be given stage presentation by amateurs upon payment of a royalty of Fifty Dollars for the first performance, and Thirty-Five Dollars for each additional performance, payable one week before the date when the play is given, to Samuel French, Inc.; at 45 West 25th Street, New York, N.Y. 10010, or at 7623 Sunset Boulevard, Hollywood, CA. 90046, or to Samuel French (Canada), Ltd. 80 Richmond Street East, Toronto, Ontario, Canada M5C 1P1.

Royalty of the required amount must be paid whether the play is presented for charity or gain and whether or not admission is charged.

Stock royalty quoted on application to Samuel French, Inc.

For all rights other than those stipulated above, apply to Samuel French, Inc.

Particular emphasis is laid on the question of amateur or professional readings, permission and terms for which must be secured in writing from Samuel French, Inc.

Copying from this book in whole or in part is strictly forbidden by law, and the right of performance is not transferable.

Whenever the play is produced the following notice must appear on all programs, printing and advertising for the play: "Produced by special arrangement with Samuel French, Inc."

Due authorship credit must be given on all programs, printing and advertising for the play.

Anyone presenting the play shall not commit or authorize any act or omission by which the copyright of the play or the right to copyright same may be impaired.

No changes shall be made in the play for the purpose of your production unless authorized in writing.

The publication of this play does not imply that it is necessarily available for performance by amateurs or professionals. Amateurs and professionals considering a production are strongly advised in their own interests to apply to Samuel French, Inc., for consent before starting rehearsals, advertising, or booking a theatre or hall.

No part of this book may be reproduced, stored in a retrieval system, or transmitted in any form, by any means, including mechanical, electronic, photocopying, recording, or otherwise, without the prior written permission of the publisher.

ISBN 0 573 68123 6   Printed in U.S.A.

IMPORTANT BILLING AND CREDIT REQUIREMENTS

All producers of AFTER CRYSTAL NIGHT must give credit to the Author of the Play in all programs distributed in connection with performances of the Play and in all instances in which the title of the Play appears for purposes of advertising, publicizing or otherwise exploiting the Play and/or a production. The name of the Author must also appear on a separate line, in which no other name appears, immediately following the title, and must appear in size of type not less than fifty percent the size of the title type.

THE MELROSE THEATRE
presents

AFTER CRYSTAL NIGHT

A New Play by
JOHN HERMAN SHANER

Directed by
COREY ALLEN

Co-Produced by
ALAN PLOTKIN

with

PHOEBE DORIN	STEVE FRANKEN
MARTIN GARNER	LEW HORN
CLAYTON LANDEY	CLAUDIA LONOW
BENJAMIN MITTLEMAN	JOSHUA SCHULMAN

DANNY WELLS

Lighting Designer	*Stage Manager*	*Costume Designer*
PAM RANK	NANCY OLIFF	PENELOPE DOUGLAS

The Melrose Theatre ● 733 N. Seward ● Hollywood

DIRECTED BY COREY ALLEN

CAST
In order of appearance

Joyce Goldstein	PHOEBE DORIN
Jerry Gardner	DANNY WELLS
Keith Goldstein	JOSHUA SCHULMAN
Seymour Goldstein	STEVE FRANKEN
Uncle Morris	MARTIN GARNER
Joe	CLAYTON LANDEY
Doug	BENJAMIN MITTLEMAN
Susana	CLAUDIA LONOW
Herbert Cohen	LEW HORN
T.V. Announcer	SCOTT ST. JAMES

The entire action of the play takes place
in the Beverly Hills home of
Mr. and Mrs. Seymour Goldstein.

The Time is the present.

ACT I
Scene I............. 5:30 on a Saturday Afternoon
Scene II............. 3:00 A.M. Sunday Morning

THERE WILL BE A 10 MINUTE INTERMISSION

ACT II
Scene I................. 9:00 A.M. Sunday Morning

UNDERSTUDIES
Margaret Serich   Steven Greenstein   Joanne Astrow

PRODUCTION STAFF
Lighting Design	PAM RANK
Costume Design	PENELOPE DOUGLAS
Stage Manager	NANCY OLIFF
Ass't Stg. Mgr.	ROGER ASKEW

MELROSE THEATRE STAFF
Founder/Artistic Director	PAUL KENT
Administrator	JOMARIE WARD
President/Theatre Designer	ELMER BLADOW
Public Relations	SUZANNE HORN
Technical Director	JOSEPH TAGGART

CAST OF CHARACTERS
(in order of appearance)

JOYCE GOLDSTEIN — *Joyce is 37, warm, intelligent, literate and politically and socially active and liberal. She is also strong willed and high strung and has somewhat of a suspicious nature. She sometimes talks almost clinically, as if she took too much psychology and sociology for her B.A. and M.A.*

JERRY GARDNER — *Jerry is 48. He dresses well, classy even, has a gold chain around his neck. Jerry is high energy, even a little eruptive. His sense of humor and his jokes are somewhat self-deprecatory, and he knows it. He smokes, eats, and drinks excessively.*

KEITH GOLDSTEIN — *Keith is quick-witted and imaginative: a sensitive looking, lively boy of 14.*

SEYMOUR GOLDSTEIN — *Seymour is 45 years old, wears glasses, of medium height, and though a little soft looking, perhaps even pudgy, he's energetic, passionate and emotional. He's had success in business which has given him what appears to be confidence. His mind is extremely quick; and like many Jews, has a very self deprecating sense of humor.*

UNCLE MORRIS — *Uncle Morris is 80, a difficult, crusty old man who, if you're kind, you say he's eccentric and if you're not, he's a little senile.*

JOE — *Joe is 28, intelligent, verbal and out spoken. He's athletic looking and once was a minor league baseball player but has done many other things since, salesman, student, generally scuffled for a living.*

DOUG — *Doug, 21, is a genuinely huge man, a street fighter, rough and powerful. He is direct and has not yet learned to censor himself.*

SUSANA — *Susana, 25, is whippet-like, intense and committed. She has rather short hair and wears a fatigue jacket.*

HERBERT COHEN — *Cohen is 55, a bit slick but ingratiating, persuasive and persistent: he is a professional fund raiser and, as most of them, has a thick skin.*

AFTER CRYSTAL NIGHT

ACT ONE
Scene 1

TIME: The present.

PLACE: Beverly Hills, California.

AT RISE: The curtain rises on the tastefully furnished, modern uncluttered living room of the Goldstein home in Beverly Hills. The floors are hardwood and stained, the paintings interesting and expensive, the furnishings are the very best. The people who live in this comfortable home are well off and organized. It's 5:30 Saturday afternoon. Sitting on a handsome sofa reading the New York Times is JOYCE GOLDSTEIN. JOYCE is 37, warm, intelligent, literate, and politically and socially active and liberal. She is also strong-willed and high strung and has somewhat of a suspicious nature. She sometimes talks almost clinically, as if she took too much psychology and sociology for her B.A. and M.A. Downstage right, JERRY GARDNER (nee Jacob Goldstein) plays a Video Game with KEITH GOLDSTEIN. JERRY has a drink in his hand, is 48. He dresses well, classy even, has a gold chain around his neck. JERRY is high energy, even a little eruptive. His sense of humor and his jokes are somewhat self-deprecatory, and he knows it. He smokes, eats, drinks excessively. KEITH is quick-witted and imaginative: a sensitive-looking, lively boy of 14. The game ends in a flurry. KEITH wins!

JERRY. Listen, wizard, remind me not to play you again, okay?

KEITH. *(Draws imaginary six-shooters.)* Pow! Pow! The Silicon Valley Kid.

JERRY. Do you beat your father?

KEITH. I let him win.

JERRY. You're a good son. *(He gets up, finishes his drink, goes to liquor cabinet, makes another; to JOYCE.)* I'm surprised he went.

JOYCE. The Lodge sent him.

JERRY. Seymour's only the Treasurer.

JOYCE. The President doesn't like them. He wanted someone fair to go.

JERRY. He shouldn't accommodate so much.

JOYCE. Seymour asked you, you didn't go.

JERRY. I worked till twenty minutes ago.

JOYCE. Uh-huh.

JERRY. All right, I wasn't working. I'm a Tax Consultant. You think I want my clients audited by the I.R.S.?

JOYCE. Just your clients?

JERRY. Me they audit automatically.

KEITH. You want to play me again, Uncle Jerry?

JERRY. No. You always win. Even the odds.

KEITH. I'll take a dive.

JERRY. That's fair. *(He heads for KEITH and the Video Game, gets ready to play.)* Hey, they ever catch that kid?

KEITH. Naa, he was from off-campus.

JERRY. Why'd he take a swipe at you, Your-Ugliness?

KEITH. Beats the shit out of me.

JOYCE. Keith!

JERRY. Must've been messing around with his woman.

KEITH. Big-John-Studd. *(JERRY and KEITH laugh.)*

(Just then the front door opens and SEYMOUR GOLDSTEIN enters. SEYMOUR, who's carrying a hat, is 45 years old, wears glasses, of medium height, and though a little soft looking, perhaps even pudgy, he's energetic, passionate and emotional. He's had success in business which has given him what appears to be confidence. His mind is extremely quick; and like many Jews, has a very self-deprecating sense of humor. He closes the front door carefully and locks it, and comes downstage into room. He moves carefully when he walks, as if not to disturb anything or anybody. SEYMOUR busses JOYCE on the cheek, waves hello to KEITH.)

KEITH. Hi, Dad.

SEYMOUR. Hello, Keith. You staying for dinner, Jacob?

JERRY. *(nod)* I invited myself. Jerry.

SEYMOUR. Jerry. Sorry. *(to JOYCE)* Why do I get picked for these things?

JOYCE. So?

SEYMOUR. *(a depreciating gesture)* Ahhh...

JERRY. I could've told you that. In fact, I did.

SEYMOUR. Hey, they wanted a first-hand report. Should the B'nai B'rith invite them to speak or not?

KEITH. You want to play me, Dad?

SEYMOUR. Maybe later. You want to play me, better practice.

KEITH. Why?

SEYMOUR. 'Cause I always beat you, that's why.

JOYCE. Uncle Morris called. Something about his checks.

SEYMOUR. Again? What's the matter with him?

JERRY. He fell off his ice truck once too often. Hey, you remember, the man got that crazy thing against furniture. Poor Aunt Harriet. She had to sit in her living room on a park bench.

SEYMOUR. *(to JOYCE)* It's true.

JOYCE. What're you going to report?

SEYMOUR. They're a bunch of lunatics.

JOYCE. The Rabbi says they're a passing phenomenon, an aberration of the times. He wouldn't let them speak at the synagogue either.

SEYMOUR. The Rabbi's a schmuck.

JOYCE. Seymour!

SEYMOUR. You said so yourself.

JOYCE. Oh, well, in that case. *(They chuckle.)*

SEYMOUR. No, I mean, remember? When he invited the Black Panthers to the Temple? And what happens? They cursed us, called us honky Jew bastards, up against the wall motherfuckers — Then asked the congregation for donations.

JOYCE. You gave also, Seymour.

SEYMOUR. *(Shrugs wryly.)* I'm a schmuck, too ... I was afraid they'd burn down the Temple.

JOYCE. Keith, darling. If you're hungry, why don't you get something to eat?

KEITH. I'm not hungry.

JOYCE. Dinner's going to be a while.

KEITH. That's OK.

JOYCE. Keith.

KEITH. Sent to the showers. *(Reluctantly KEITH clicks off Video Game. There's an imperceptible pause as JOYCE waits for him to exit; SEYMOUR notices it.)*

JOYCE. No, really. What if someone saw you at a JDL meeting? Thought you were a crazy militant?

JERRY. Seymour, the militant.

JOYCE. Well, still ... a Business Manager depends on good will. You think your clients'll do business with people associated with militants? No way.

SEYMOUR. It was a beat up schul in a rundown neighborhood, like the kind you came from, a storefront. Paper yarmulkes in cardboard boxes. Nobody we know ever goes near there.

JOYCE. Okay. Fine. I just hope nobody recognized you and we don't have a lot of explaining, uh, that we're not misunderstood.

SEYMOUR. I told you, I'm not afraid of that! *(slight pause)* Besides, I sat very low, behind a pole, and pulled my hat way down. *(gets hat)* The one you bought me, for New York. It's a size too big.

JERRY. Was the F.B.I. there? They love those meetings. They take pictures.

SEYMOUR. Hey, let them take. Look at this hat. *(Pulls on*

hat and indeed it's way too big, almost down to his eyebrows.)

JOYCE. Don't joke, Seymour. Sheila Weintraub told me the F.B.I. infiltrated her Hadassah chapter.

SEYMOUR. Come on, I listened to a few wild speeches and came home.

JOYCE. I'll make some coffee.

SEYMOUR. Naa, I had some already.

JOYCE. Oh? With whom?

SEYMOUR. Uh, well, see...

JOYCE. *(She stops.)* You had coffee with them??

SEYMOUR. De Caf. Coffee makes me nervous lately.

JOYCE. Seymour.

SEYMOUR. They went out after. *(shrugs)* They dragged me with them.

JOYCE. You made an eloquent speech against them at the Lodge, you said they had the mentality of a street gang and you had coffee with them.

SEYMOUR. Okay, okay, how else could I make an informed judgment? See if they were normal.

JOYCE. The Lodge applauded your speech. *I* applauded your speech. And I'm your toughest critic.

SEYMOUR. No—o. You're my toughest critic? I didn't know that.

JOYCE. You're not mine?

JERRY. So? Are they normal?

SEYMOUR. *(speculatively)* Umm...

JERRY. What'd they do, beat up the restaurant owner?

SEYMOUR. We're in the deli, see, people are talking, discussing, well, not exactly discussing, *yelling;* then a JDL nut, a dark little guy, a brisket sandwich in his hand, jumps up, he's arguing with somebody, not me. I'm quiet. But he turns on me, shouts in *my* face, "Never again, never again." I hadn't said one word to him. And now he's got a mouthful of brisket, and he's yelling at me! Mind you, people are looking and everything. I'm embarrassed, I'm...

JERRY. Deli owner should've kicked them out.

SEYMOUR. Yeah. He came over; he wouldn't let them pay for anything, not that they tried very hard. The neighborhood's changing, he had trouble. They did something for him. I don't know what.

JOYCE. You didn't mention anything, did you?

SEYMOUR. *(He grimaces, gestures as to say, of course not, don't be foolish.)* Deli owner put his arm around them. *(Chuckles ironically.)* Me too, he thought I was one of them ... Then all of them, all right, not all of them, I want to be fair, *some* of them are banging knives, forks against cups, plates, tabletops, shouting and yelling, "Never again, never again." "Fuck Vanessa Redgrave" ... I have to tell the Lodge. They're very excitable.

JOYCE. What did you do?

SEYMOUR. I didn't know what to do, so I ordered a salami sandwich.

JOYCE. What's your recommendations?

SEYMOUR. Why should we give them a platform? They go against all the Jewish principles I grew up with.

JERRY. You know what the F.B.I. has now? Voice prints. You shouldn't've talked!

SEYMOUR. *(quietly)* Jacob, what are you doing?

JERRY. I told you a million times, Jerry, Jerry. Not Jacob.

SEYMOUR. My brother *Jacob's* still angry because he wasn't born Protestant.

JERRY. It *used* to be Protestant; this is L.A., so now I want to be born Hispanic.

SEYMOUR. You came over to aggravate me, right?

JERRY. What else is a brother for?

(Suddenly, they hear the back door rattle; someone's trying to get in! SEYMOUR, JOYCE, JERRY freeze, listen. Again, the sounds of someone, louder this time, trying to break in!)

SEYMOUR. Shh ... What's that?

JERRY. Someone's trying to get in the back door.

JOYCE. *(Moves toward back door as we hear more door tampering.)* Get away from there. We called the police!

UNCLE MORRIS. *(O.S.)* What do you mean, get away from there?

JOYCE. Uncle Morris!

UNCLE MORRIS. *(O.S.)* You're chasing me away?!

JOYCE. You've got to stop doing this.

UNCLE MORRIS. *(O.S.)* An Ice Man comes in the back.

SEYMOUR. You're not an Ice Man anymore.

UNCLE MORRIS. To who? To you? To *me*, I'm still an Ice Man.

(UNCLE MORRIS has appeared on stage. He's 80, a difficult, crusty old man who, if you're kind, you say he's eccentric and if you're not, a little senile.)

UNCLE MORRIS. *(to SEYMOUR)* Your back door is stuck.

JERRY. Not stuck. *Locked.*

UNCLE MORRIS. Ah ha, look who's here. *Jacob Goldstein.*

JERRY. *(Pissed, he makes an about-face away from his UNCLE MORRIS; turns back.)* Jerry Gardner, Uncle Morris.

UNCLE MORRIS. *(to SEYMOUR, JOYCE and the world)* He fixed his nose, he changed his name, God forbid he should bargain — listen, are you still circumcized?

JERRY. For the moment. Then I'm going to this new plastic surgeon in Beverly Hills. Born Again Foreskins!

UNCLE MORRIS. *(to SEYMOUR and JOYCE)* You see, *you* don't believe him. But *I* believe him.

JERRY. No wonder Jewish men are neurotic, the minute you come into the world, they cut off a quarter of your pecker.

UNCLE MORRIS. In your case, three-quarters.

JOYCE. Uncle Morris!

UNCLE MORRIS. All right, a half.

JERRY. The man's senile.

UNCLE MORRIS. How's the Korean woman on Olympic Boulevard? This time he's looking for a Korean wife. Find one yet? *(Makes face.)* I hear the women have small behinds. *(Gestures a wide girth.)* I like a good "tuchus."

JERRY. The man should be put away in a *home.*

UNCLE MORRIS. No *homes.* What did your father say on his death bed? That you should both take care of me in my old age. Forever.

JERRY. Still falling off the ice truck, huh, Uncle Morris?

UNCLE MORRIS. No, it's not the ice truck anymore. I'm

just senile now. *(wry)* But as I get older, my senile gets better. Where's Keith? He's alright? *(SEYMOUR nods, comes back from bar with a whiskey for UNCLE MORRIS.)* Well, what did you want me to come here for?

SEYMOUR. Come here for ... You called *us*, Uncle Morris.

UNCLE MORRIS. What did I want? ... *(wry)* Well, maybe my senile isn't getting better after all. *(He drinks a schnaps.)* Now I remember. The money, that's why I came over, my support.

SEYMOUR. We always mail it to you.

UNCLE MORRIS. No. They need it.

SEYMOUR. Who needs it?

UNCLE MORRIS. The Irgun.

JERRY. *(patiently)* Morris, the Irgun disbanded forty years ago.

UNCLE MORRIS. Oh. Yeah, that's right. I have hardening of the arteries. That means blood travels up to the head, but only now and again. I don't mean the Irgun, I mean my Ketzellas.

JERRY. You mean you're saving my support for the *cats?*

UNCLE MORRIS. Listen, my Ketzellas call me more often than you do.

JERRY. The cats??

UNCLE MORRIS. Why not? My wife's dead, I got no children, I got no relatives, so I'm giving it to them.

JERRY. Wait a minute. What am I? Chopped liver? *(to JOYCE and SEYMOUR)* He's forgotten we're his relatives.

UNCLE MORRIS. What should I do? Give you your

money *back?* It would only make you feel guilty.

JERRY. You're going to a home! Cats!

SEYMOUR. Jerry, he's teasing you. With food prices now, how can he live on Social Security? *(SEYMOUR and JERRY take out check books.)*

UNCLE MORRIS. Oh—no? There's a lot of widows, right. They all sit on bus stops on Fairfax. I take a nice shave. I put on a little witch hazel, I walk along the street, without my cane; that's it brother! The widows invite me for lunch, for supper; why not? I'm a catch.

JERRY. Boy, oh boy, a catch.

UNCLE MORRIS. Certainly, I'm alive, ain't I?! Those old birds are still interested. They all take Percodan, it makes 'em excited. But since my prostate operation I can't do anything. *(conspiratorially)* So I don't tell 'em nothin' 'til after I eat. Where's my money? *(The brothers shake their heads but obediently finish making out checks.)*

SEYMOUR. *(handing him a check)* You come here, insult us, and ask for money?

UNCLE MORRIS. That's right. And you give it to me, don't you? *(UNCLE MORRIS plucks the check from JERRY's hand.)* You're a schmuck.

JERRY. Thank you.

UNCLE MORRIS. *(Plucks check from SEYMOUR's hand.)* And you're a nebish. Your father had no luck. *(The old man trundles toward back door.)*

SEYMOUR. Use the front door, Uncle Morris. The police'll mistake you for a prowler.

UNCLE MORRIS. An Ice Man uses only back doors.

(We hear the back door slam. SEYMOUR sighs.)

JOYCE. Don't sigh, Seymour.
SEYMOUR. I'm not sighing.

(The front doorbell rings and JOYCE crosses, opens door slightly but remains standing there.)

JOYCE. *(surprised)* Uh ... yes?
MALE VOICE. Is Seymour Goldstein here?
JOYCE. Yes...
MALE VOICE. We'd like to see him.
JOYCE. Uh ... Who shall I say is calling?
MALE VOICE. Tell him the people he had coffee with.
JOYCE. Coffee with...? Coffee! *Seymour! Come quick!*

(SEYMOUR has risen quickly, quizzically comes to the door. Startled, he opens the door wider, and two very big young men and a young woman enter. They are JOE, DOUG and SUSANA. JOE is 28, intelligent, verbal and outspoken. He's athletic looking and once was a minor league baseball player but has done many other things since, salesman, student, generally scuffled for a living. DOUG, 21, is a genuinely huge man, a street fighter, rough and powerful. He is direct and has not yet learned to censor himself. SUSANA, 25, is whippet-like, intense and committed. She has rather short hair and wears a fatigue jacket.)

SEYMOUR. Oh. Hi. Uh, what are you doing here, fellas?
JOE. We looked for you at the deli but you'd split. *(They come in.)*
SEYMOUR. *(Stands at the door a moment as the JDL move in*

room. Then he closes door.) Uh ... this is my wife, Joyce, my brother, Jerry.

JOE. Mrs. Goldstein, I'm Joe. That's Doug.

DOUG. Mrs.

JOE. And Susana.

SEYMOUR. How'd you know where I lived?

JOE. You signed the guest list.

SEYMOUR. Oh. *(louder, for JOYCE's benefit)* Everybody else did, too.

JOE. You mentioned your son's school.

JOYCE. Seymour!

SEYMOUR. *(Studiously, he does not acknowledge.)* School's taking care of it.

JOE. Keith all right?

SEYMOUR. He wasn't really involved.

JOE. Uh-huh. You mentioned it, so we're here. *(JOYCE throws SEYMOUR a scalding look.)*

DOUG. They found leaflets in some lockers.

SEYMOUR. The Anti-Defamation League's on top of it.

SUSANA. Uh-huh. They do good work; at what they do.

JOE. *(He gives SUSANA a look.)* Susana.

JOYCE. Seymour, really, dinner's almost ready.

DOUG. You want we should talk to the principal?

JOYCE. God forbid!

SEYMOUR. It's behind us, let's forget it. Listen, fellas, we eat very early on Saturday.

JOE. Sure. I understand. Some crazies. They've been hitting schools.

DOUG. Your Lodge should hear us.

SEYMOUR. Well, maybe some other time, you never know.

JOE. Seymour, there was talk about a donation, remember?

SEYMOUR. Who talked?

DOUG. We did. But you were definitely in the conversation.

SEYMOUR. When?

SUSANA. When you were yelling in the Deli.

SEYMOUR. No, it was for a salami sandwich.

SUSANA. You didn't have your checkbook, you said.

JOE. A lot of people promise, you know. They hear we protected a cemetery, creeps are always turning over gravestones at Jewish cemeteries. *(Snorts ruefully.)* You ever hear anybody turning them over at Catholic cemeteries? Or they hear we busted some Black dudes harassing old folks on Fairfax, so they get excited. They say they want to give, but you know people. They forget quick.

DOUG. A lot of wives talk their husbands out of it when they get home, so we learned to pick up checks when the body's warm. Not you, Mrs. Goldstein. *Other* wives.

(KEITH, eating a piece of cheese, is drawn by the presence of strangers in the house, edges into room.)

JOYCE. *(She notices.)* Keith, darling, please finish that in the kitchen.

KEITH. *(Rather than go he pops the cheese in his mouth, finishes in one swallow.)* Hi guys.

JOE. Keith. *(Palm up, DOUG puts out a huge paw and*

KEITH responds with a High Five.) That kid at school, why'd he pick you? *(KEITH shrugs, I don't know.)*

SUSANA. You have a tote bag? *(KEITH nods.)* Bet your name's on it.

KEITH. *(nods)* They all look alike...

JOE. Goldstein.

KEITH. Yeah. K. Goldstein. Velcroed. *(JOE glances at SEYMOUR and JOYCE.)*

SEYMOUR. Well, perhaps we'll talk some other time, so thanks for coming over, maybe you'll call me at the office.

JOE. Seymour. Listen to me. You were at the meeting. There's something alive there.

SEYMOUR. No, no. There's nothing alive there. I mean, it was for the *Lodge*.

JOE. Alive! You know we're strapped. We run an office, we have phones, patrols, we need two-way radios.

DOUG. Old ladies on the street with Pishka boxes don't make it for us.

SUSANA. It's for you too, Seymour.

SEYMOUR. Listen, I know, but ... Please, don't play on my sympathies.

JOE. Okay then, go with the essentials in a philosophy. Can you dig self-defense?

SEYMOUR. But you're a violent group. I mean, you're vigilantes. I don't go with that!

JERRY. *(A little scared of them, takes a step in.)* I agree with my brother! *(They turn back to him. He takes a quick step back.)* Okay, I'll pledge one hundred dollars. *(JOE gives him a look.)* I'd love to sit and smooze with you guys. And Miss.

But I have an engagement.

JOYCE. *(innocently)* I thought you were staying for supper.

SEYMOUR. Jerry! *(JERRY mouths "I'll call you later. Good luck." He gives his sister-in-law a look and exits.)*

JOYCE. Sure you're strapped for money; you throw a pipe bomb here and a pipe bomb there. You fight in the streets! We've lived all these years because we used our heads.

SEYMOUR. JDL t-shirts, strutting around with baseball bats and nunchucks, that's not a Jewish image.

JOE. Look, we're on the streets to stop goons hurting us. You think you can reason with those people? God knows the Jews've tried long enough, and they've got the hook in their throat every time, face it. Please don't ignore the fears, the anxieties of poor people in our neighborhoods, our kids in city schools, old people left behind when sons and daughters split to the suburbs. Hey, old parents don't move to the hills, or the beaches or the mountains. They're lost there. They can't shop there. They can't bullshit with the yentas there, so they're stuck. Hey, there's a bunch of old Yids still want to go to synagogue, sue me, we got to walk 'em over and walk 'em back. Otherwise, the brutes rob 'em, then for who the hell knows why, kill 'em. That's the reality, man. And the minute some Jews fight back, they call it *Vigilantism*. That's the buzzword. When we fight back, they describe our resistance as agression. Yeah. We're violent. When someone's *violent* on us.

JOYCE. No, you may've started out that way, but now you're the Jewish *Offense* League.

DOUG. Hey, we catch 'em painting swastikas on our buildings, yeah, we're gonna mess 'em up. Then call the cops. They take 'em to court. You think the court's dealing with it? Watch the six o'clock news.

SUSANA. Have you tried the cops lately? You dial an emergency, you hold twenty minutes listening to Muzak!

SEYMOUR. You put the word Jewish in front of Defense League, you're saying you represent me. I never elected you a leader. We have capable, qualified people to act for us!

JOE. People are scared. When we're on Fairfax, they feel a little safer, not much, but a little. Hey, Mr. Goldstein, with all due respect, you're sitting in Beverly Hills. You don't live in the urban badlands where community organization and law enforcement's weak. That's what's so cruel. In the past, vigilante groups were led by the frontier elite — by those who had the most money, by those who had the most to lose. Do we look like the elite to you? Doug's a brick layer. Susana's a high school P.E. teacher laid off.

SUSANA. I spent too much time hanging out with these guys.

DOUG. Naa, you were recruiting kids at school

JOE. And I'm trying to get a falafel stand going. You know what my mother keeps saying to me? You were a hippie, a yippie, why can't you at least become a Yuppie.

SUSANA. My mother says I'll forget about all this if I just get married.

DOUG. My mother doesn't talk to me at all.

JOE. We're not the lawyers and doctors and big merchants, okay. We're waiting for them to join us. It's the suburban elite who are the most aloof because on an everyday basis, they are the least threatened, the most secure. But that's changing too. You know what they call a Jewish liberal? Somebody whose son hasn't been beaten up yet.

JOYCE. Look, there are no pogroms out there. We have the Constitution, the Bill of Rights, and that's what's safeguarding us. Not you. What am I gonna do? Tell my husband to grab a gun at the first sight of an anti-Semite and shoot him?

SUSANA. After the Holocaust, Jews have a moral obligation to anti-Semites to be powerful so as never to tempt them to such behavior again.

SEYMOUR. The Jews shouldn't be blamed for anything. The JDL doesn't have a plan. My Lodge has a plan. The B'nai B'rith has a plan, and the plan is gather all their propaganda, have constant surveillance over them!

JOE. It's inconceivable not to have a nucleus of capable men and women who could organize and respond in case of an emergency. Come on. After Crystal Night?

SEYMOUR. This is not Poland. This is not Germany, 1939. The parallels are not there. Yes, we have nuts here, but the FBI's watching them, the IRS's watching them. Professionals! Not people running around looking to get headlines for themselves. Let the proper authorities take care of it!

JOE. You're right. I can't name ten Jews that were killed because they were Jews, but I'll tell you a couple million who always have to worry about those bastards, who are on constant internal alert; the damaged guys who hear those bastards echo way out in the distance so they bend themselves out of shape not to be identified. We are constantly recovering from one kind of assault or another. Graffiti here, a Farrakhan there, they kill Alan Berg in Denver. And not only from outside enemies. We are great self-executioners. The Jews've been twisted. If you want to straighten them out, you have to bend them hard in the other direction.

JOYCE. You had to ask.

SEYMOUR. I didn't have to ask. He was going to tell us anyway.

JOE. Let me speak to your Lodge, Seymour. Look what happened at your kid's school.

SEYMOUR. Leave us alone! Why do we have to go through this? The Lodge did already. I did already. Please!

JOE. I know, I know you don't want to think about it. I didn't either. Are you kidding? I was raised a Jewish Wasp. All the Jews I knew were convinced they had to masquerade as anything but a Jew. Whatever JDL's faults, and they got plenty, that's not one of them. My father was so guarded about his background he never let me meet his relatives. We celebrated Christmas and Easter dinner, ham with specks of dried cherries on top. I went to an Episcopalian prep school, I sang hymns during the mandatory chapel service. You want to hear crazy? I once brought home, by accident, a bottle of Dr. Brown's Celery Tonic for dinner, and I swear to God my father got scared I was becoming too ethnic. God forbid I should've brought home a bottle of *seltzer*. One of the

JDL-niks took me to Kol Nidre. I burst into tears. I had never heard it before, but it came back to me from somewhere. Metaphysical, right? My parents blew it, they blew the treasure, the fortune of Jewish learning, of history, of culture. They squandered the importance of family life. The miraculous pauses of great holidays and ceremonies; Sabbath, the white tablecloth, the candles, the singing. The unusual duration of Jewish history, the extraordinary originality of Hebraic thought, its astonishing impact on the world, that marvelous past. And I knew nothing about it. I had historical amnesia, I had marched and fought for every movement, every cause, except a Jewish cause. That I was ashamed of. That wasn't hip enough for the room. Jewishness was a secret source of terror for me. Wow! Now I'm reclaiming my amputated past, fighting for it, making waves, not being silent, wild and loud and swinging back.

Doug. Let Joe speak to your Lodge, Seymour. They'll like him. Then you'll see. That'll break the ice, then the other Lodges'll let him speak too. *(Nods toward JOE.)* Isn't he great?

Seymour. Listen, I don't believe our security lies in taking the law into our own hands. That kind of simplistic approach to complicated problems — you know what it produces? Battling groups, wild antagonisms, not solutions.

Joe. We want solutions, but survival comes first.

Seymour. But you're polarizing the community.

Joe. What about giving them options?!

Joyce. You blow up a few isolated incidents, way out of proportion, for your own purposes. Scare tactics. Is it to panic people? Do you raise money from it or what? Who asked for your protection? The Jewish Community doesn't need it or want it. Para-military operations, appeals to raw emotions, terrific, listen to some of the stuff you just spewed. I'm sorry. I think you're a potential danger. Where do you people come from? Who gives you the right? You give yourself a Jewish name and you act in the name of the Jews?

SUSANA. We're a danger?

JOYCE. Yes!

SUSANA. You and your Juliette Nails. And your clothes, everything's got to have a name on it, and what's your job? Shopping, lunch, and body wraps! And you know where your synagogue is, where you go to pray? It's on Rodeo Drive, next door to Gucci's. Or is it Pucci's, I forgot!

JOYCE. *(Thrusts out hands.)* Do you see Juliette Nails, Miss!!?

SUSANA. Ms., lady, Ms.

JOYCE. Och! You give us a bad name.

SUSANA. You *gave* us a bad name.

JOYCE. Hooligan!

SUSANA. J.A.P. *(JOYCE stomps away, so does SUSANNA.)*

DOUG. Yeah. This shit really gets people riled up.

SEYMOUR. I'm proud I made money. I'm proud my wife wears nice clothes. That's right! I am not going to apologize to anyone for that! I worked hard, I did well. No guilt trips! We're going to live here forever! What do you want me to do, make Aliyah to Israel and pick oranges?

JOYCE. If you had a JDL convention, you could hold it in a phone booth. And I'll bet two or three in the booth'd be police informers. Seymour, could we please have supper?!

JOE. Susanna!

SUSANA. I'm sorry, Joe ... I'm sorry, Mr. Goldstein, I apologize, Mrs. Goldstein.

JOYCE. I don't even have a mink coat!

SUSANA. Okay, okay.

JOYCE. Do I have a mink coat?

SEYMOUR. No, no ... I don't believe this; I mean, if you guys are so right, so terrific, you have all the answers — why are most Jews against you?

JOE. Most Jews I don't know, you ask me they're closet sympathizers. Only they think they have to be nicer, better than everybody else. Don't make waves or what will the Christians say, what will the Christians think. But the Jewish Establishment I know. Hey, they're a multimillion dollar concern, afraid we'll take some of their membership, some of their statistics and some of their *money*. All we want is for them not to be such limp dicks like they were in the 30's and 40's. *(Fishes out a folded leaflet, almost slaps it into SEYMOUR's hand.)* Here. Maybe this'll help you figure things out.

SEYMOUR. *(Scans it, folds it, gives it back to JOE.)* You're going down there? *(JOE nods. SEYMOUR takes the folded leaflet back from JOE, hands it to JOYCE.)* How many you going?

JOE. As many as'll come. Thirty, forty, maybe.

SEYMOUR. How many of *them* show up?

JOE. About fifty, sixty, sometimes more, sometimes less.

JOYCE. *(Unfolds the leaflet, reads out loud.)* "The sixteenth." That's tomorrow. "The American Nazi Party announces its National Convention, Republic Auditorium. Los Angeles, California. Two P.M. Heil Hitler." *Uch...*

SEYMOUR. Jesus, who the hell'd rent to them?

JOE. The Republic's owned by a Jew. He's renting it to them.

SEYMOUR. Come on! *(JOE picks up phone, hands it to SEYMOUR, who doesn't take it.)*

JOYCE. I don't believe you, you people always exaggerate.

JOE. *(Proffers phone again, now to her.)* Ask for Sam Rubin.

JOYCE. *(not taking phone)* Well ... Sam Rubin isn't necessarily a Jewish name. *(to SEYMOUR)* Weren't you in the Army with a William Levy, and *he* wasn't Jewish?

SEYMOUR. That's right!

JOE. Hey, Seymour, a donation at least for the bail.

SEYMOUR. There'll be arrests?

JOE. *(shrugs)* They see us, we see them, pow, that's it. *(Looks at SEYMOUR's face.)* Don't be depressed. We're used to it.

SEYMOUR. *(Sighs deeply.)* Uh ... you guys want a drink or something? Some schnapps, vodka, whatever, a cognac?

DOUG. Could I have tea with lemon?

SEYMOUR. Tea with lemon??

DOUG. Yeah.

SEYMOUR. Tea with lemon.

DOUG. Yeah! Tea with lemon! You never heard of tea

with lemon!

SEYMOUR. Yeah, sure. But I just thought *you* guys...

JOE. Okay, give me *(Plays macho.) Bull* malt liquor *beer.* *(This gets a laugh even from JOYCE. SEYMOUR heads to kitchen, but JOYCE gestures she'll go.)*

JOYCE. What can I get you, Miss?

SUSANA. Tea with lemon's fine. Not white sugar, though. Honey. *(JOYCE throws her a look, exits to kitchen.)*

SEYMOUR. *(to JOE)* This is the way you expect to raise money?

JOE. *(at SUSANA)* Yeah, that's always been a problem for us.

SEYMOUR. *(Lowers voice so it doesn't carry to kitchen and a note of braggadocio creeps into it.)* When I was a kid I didn't run away you know. I was a scrapper. Just because I'm older now and out of shape now, don't think I can't handle myself.

JOE. Come on down then.

JOYCE. *(Enters carrying a beer on a platter.)* Come down where?

DOUG. The Nazi rally, to the fight.

JOYCE. *(Almost drops the platter.)* What?!! A fight??! Seymour!

SEYMOUR. Nothing! They're going to protest. We were talking. Hypothetical. Please! *(to JOE)* But there are police, aren't there police keeping you apart?

SUSANA. It's cops you watch out for. They pile in with their clubs swinging.

DOUG. Yeah, but one good thing about the cops. They hit everybody they can. They're not prejudiced.

JOYCE. If you wouldn't go, there wouldn't be any trouble.

JOE. Look, all we know is, if you're pushing Jews around, we're going to bust your head. Let them know Jewish blood doesn't come cheap. We're tired of that shit. We're not big speech makers, big thinkers, looking for love from everybody. Hey, the Blacks got their Uncle Toms, we got our Uncle Jakes. We need some schtarkers in the street, you know what I'm saying? The Jewish Establishment makes speeches, that's cool. Maybe it does some good. But when Moses saw an Egyptian beating the shit out of a Jew, he didn't call a meeting or debate the pros and cons of that Hebrew getting whipped. He didn't make a speech. Moses smote the son of a bitch. You dig what smote means? That cat got what he deserved.

DOUG. See, I can dig Moses, I know where he's coming from, he didn't turn the other cheek, 'cause if he'd turned the other cheek like all the rest of the Jews, they'd a roasted his ass in Auschwitz too. I'm jumping a couple of thousand years, but you get my meaning.

SEYMOUR. Oh, God, I know, I know, but look how easy this gets out of hand. How close to the surface the beast in us waits. He doesn't need much to erupt. That's why we are a people of the Law. That's what Torah means. Law. You swing bats and fists, but you don't know that. But our prophets, they knew that. They had inspired insight, they really did. They realized we needed something better than just crashing down on each other's skulls. If man was inclined to do that, something had to evolve, to work it out of his system. The Law. You talked about Moses.

Okay, but there was another Moses, a later Moses, he's my man too. When he came down from Sinai, he didn't come down with a clenched fist in a Star of David. He came down with a tablet of Law!

SUSANA. Nobody's ever gonna tattoo a number on my arm like they did my father.

JOE. Advocating genocide's not free speech. It's crying *fire* in a crowded theatre. No, man, Nazis march carrying placards "Burn the Jews" without somebody confronting them? — No way.

JOYCE. That's what they want. What are you going to do? Stir up monsters that only beg to be aroused? *Don't* give them publicity!

JOE. You think if they get publicity, the masses'll rush to join them in lock step, that coverage'll get followers. You suspect, you fear that what they have to sell has millions of buyers out there, hungry and waiting.

SEYMOUR. Who knows? Is anybody sure? Why take chances like that?

JOE. These monsters can't stand the light, it's better calling them out, expose them, deal with them. The larger society understands and *respects* that. Who says cancer gets better when you pretend it's not there?

SEYMOUR. There are tens of thousands of sickies out there. Their dollars, the size of their meetings shoot up, they thrive on violence, confrontation, *TV coverage!*

JOE. Hey, maybe it'll just scare potential members, who knows? Make 'em think before they join. They're used to hitting Jews without us hitting back.

DOUG. Now they know they can get busted heads *too*. Is that bad?

SUSANA. That's not bad.

DOUG. *Yeah!* Let Nazis be afraid of *us* for a change! *(He bangs a giant fist that rattles the pedestal coffee table. JOYCE steadies the quivering glass.)*

JOE. The Convention's not for you, okay, I understand that. Bail's going to be huge on this one, their topic is, "Jews as Toxic Waste. Where to Dump It." *Just help with money.*

SEYMOUR. I didn't say it's not for me. You're saying it's not for me.

JOE. Hey, great! Then it's for you!

SEYMOUR. Are you crazy?

DOUG. Another one bites the dust. V'yiskadal V'yiskadash.

SEYMOUR. If I wanted, I'd come down. But, uh, this is my busy season anyway.

SUSANA. Hey, if they come for us again, you'll go with them again. Nice Jewish boys. Paralyzed ball-less wonders. God, I can't stand nice Jewish boys.

JOE. Listen, Susana. Would you wait for me outside?

SUSANA. I'll be cool.

JOE. You're not coming along anymore!

SUSANA. Okay! Okay! I'll just keep my mouth shut. *(to SEYMOUR)* Seymour, we need your money bad, and Joe's gonna kick my ass later, but please: my busy season? You insult me. Hey, I'd like to meet Mr. Right too. I want to be a Yuppie also and drive a Bronco but priorities, Seymour, priorities.

DOUG. *(The towering man moves SUSANA out of harms way.)* Hey, there's this writer? He's rich like you,

Seymour, but he still comes down. Says it makes him a better writer. He's a little weird.

JOE. But he fights. *(DOUG grunts in admiration, gives the clenched fist salute.)*

SUSANA. We went to see his movies. His name was right on the screen! *(sadly)* Gee, they were lousy.

JOE. Yeah, but he bails himself out.

DOUG. That's the only good thing about his movies.

JOE. See? All kinds contribute: Lawyers, doctors, writers, businessmen like yourself. So what do you say?

SEYMOUR. Listen, I admire some of the things you guys do, standing up to Farrakhan at his mosque, but mostly I ... you're too ... But ... uh, let me think about it. Let me talk it over with my wife.

SUSANA. Then we won't-get-anything.

JOE. Susana, goddamnit!

SUSANA. *(quickly)* I apologize, Mrs. Goldstein. I apologize.

JOE. I'll come back tomorrow, okay?

SEYMOUR. *(much too happily)* You're going? *(JOE laughs ruefully; the JDL head to the door; they wave goodbye to KEITH who goes up to his room. The JDL exits.)*

JOYCE. *(the instant the door closes)* You weren't going to say anything!

SEYMOUR. Well ... I didn't tell them *which* school.

JOYCE. Don't make a thing out of it we said, let it blow over. We all talked it through, Seymour.

SEYMOUR. All right, all right, it just came out.

JOYCE. Now they'll come to the school. They'll make a mountain out of a molehill. They'll *picket*. Oh, God, they love to picket. With bullhorns, Seymour. *(SEYMOUR feels the folded leaflet in his back pocket, taps it on his hand and sighs.)* Don't sigh, Seymour... Throw it away. *(He tosses the leaflet into the waste basket next to the bar.)*

(KEITH enters.)

SEYMOUR. *(Gestures toward the door.)* You saw them?
KEITH. Sure.
SEYMOUR. That's it?
KEITH. Well, I'd like that big guy sitting next to me at school.
SEYMOUR. Uh-huh...
KEITH. Dad, I don't know about that stuff.
SEYMOUR. Yeah.
KEITH. That's for you guys.
SEYMOUR. Yeah, maybe.
KEITH. *(reassuringly)* Everybody's forgot that school thing, Dad. *(Pantomimes hitting a long drive into the stands for a home run.)* That-ball's-history! *(Pleased and vindicated, JOYCE gestures to SEYMOUR: See, I told you, it's cool. SEYMOUR nods acceptance.)* That was one big dude though.
JOYCE. I thought he was going to break the coffee table.
KEITH. *(examining the coffee table)* Gee, he did.
JOYCE. *(Steps quickly to coffee table.)* No!
KEITH. Putting you on. I'm only putting you on. I'm going over to David's. *(He scoots up the stairs to his room, exits. SEYMOUR collects the New York Times.)*
JOYCE. I don't want them back.

SEYMOUR. Um.

(The doorbell rings and JOYCE answers.)

JOYCE. Oh, Mr. Cohen.

(MR. HERBERT COHEN stands in the doorway. COHEN is 55, a bit slick but ingratiating, persuasive and persistent: he is a professional fundraiser and, as most of them, has a thick skin.)

JOYCE. Seymour, it's Mr. *Cohen* from the U.J.A. *(SEYMOUR comes out of the kitchen, shakes hands with COHEN.)*
COHEN. I was in the neighborhood, I thought I'd say hello. *(They sit facing each other.)* So, how are you?
SEYMOUR. Fine.
JOYCE. Fine.
COHEN. And Keith?
JOYCE. Fine.
COHEN. Wonderful, Keith's a terrific kid. I love 'im. *(a violent gesture towards the door)* I didn't know you're involved with them!
JOYCE. *(quickly)* We're not.
COHEN. I was parking. I saw them leave.
SEYMOUR. Naa, the Lodge wanted them checked out, they're going to speak to us.
COHEN. A B'nai B'rith Lodge is letting them speak?
SEYMOUR. Well, at least I'm recommending it. *(JOYCE peers questioningly at SEYMOUR.)*
COHEN. I'm surprised.
JOYCE. I'm surprised, *too.*
COHEN. *(to JOYCE)* Did you see what they looked like?

Your Lodge won't let them speak.

SEYMOUR. We let the Black Panthers and La Raza speak.

COHEN. *(jocular)* Are you defending them?

SEYMOUR. I'm not defending them, I'm not attacking them. So, Herb, what can I do for you?

COHEN. For me? Nothing.

SEYMOUR. So, what's the matter, didn't you get my check?

COHEN. *(light)* Sure we got your check. Are you kidding? Your father-in-law's head of the drive this year, and if we didn't get a check, Gottenu.

SEYMOUR. Good.

COHEN. *(not so light)* The only thing is, how come it was so small?

SEYMOUR. What?

COHEN. You always send twice as much.

JOYCE. How much did you send, Seymour?

SEYMOUR. I sent, Joyce.

COHEN. *(to JOYCE)* After all, your father's head of the drive this year.

SEYMOUR. You told me ten times already, Mr. Cohen.

COHEN. *Mr.* Cohen? Ai, ai, ai. Listen, if that's all you can afford, that's all you can afford. What, you've been giving to *them*?

SEYMOUR. Business is slow, interest rates are up, things!

COHEN. Seymour. Please don't be so hostile. Why are you so hostile? I think *they* made you hostile. A few foolish people give them money. I really hope you're not among them. The Jewish Defense League's been repudiated by, by, *(He has his briefcase open, keeps talking as he instantly fishes out a newsletter, reads:)* The Union of American Hebrew Congregations, the American Jewish Congress, the Anti-Defamation League of B'nai B'rith.

SEYMOUR. *(interrupts, out of nowhere)* Norman Lear gave them fifty dollars.

COHEN. *(pause)* I don't believe it.

SEYMOUR. I heard Norman Lear gave them fifty dollars.

COHEN. Ohh, you heard.

SEYMOUR. He mailed it in a plain envelope, but he gave.

COHEN. Seymour, you're a sensible man, only Jewish *fascists* give to them and Norman Lear is a big liberal, he's practically a Communist.

SEYMOUR. Only fascists, huh. Fascists. *I* gave to them!

COHEN. Well, not *you,* you're not a fascist, don't be foolish. You're just misguided ... How much did you give?

SEYMOUR. Plenty!

JOYCE. Plenty??

SEYMOUR. Well, not plenty, but, Herb, you're really getting on my nerves, so please...

COHEN. Okay. Listen, just let me read you this, can I read you this?

SEYMOUR. I'd rather you didn't.

COHEN. *(miffed, a little uncomprehending)* You don't want me to read you the bulletin of the Jewish Federation Council of Greater Los Angeles?

SEYMOUR. Not right now.

COHEN. All right ... If you don't, you don't. *(Makes to put bulletin away, suddenly starts reading from bulletin.)* Jewish organizations throughout the United States with unanimity of opinion, have condemned the Jewish Defense League. Its actions, its statements, its tactics, are harmful and counter-productive!!

SEYMOUR. *(spiteful)* I bet Woody Allen gave!

COHEN. Woody Allen would absolutely not give! And if he gave, I'm finished with his movies. *(He puts bulletin back in briefcase, tries to lighten up.)* Now then, after hearing, I must say, that damning report, I'm certain you'll reconsider.

SEYMOUR. Yes. I will reconsider. I'm considering sending some money I usually send to the U.J.A. to the J.D.L.

COHEN. Ah-ah-ah — you sent us already.

SEYMOUR. I can always stop a check.

COHEN. You would stop a check to the U.J.A.??

SEYMOUR. Okay! Okay! You're right, the bulletin's right, my wife's right, I'm right, and they're all wrong!

COHEN. Yes! And I'll tell you, as much as I love you, and your dear wife and children *and* your father-in-law, who I might add is *chairman* of this year's drive.

SEYMOUR. *(Jumps up.)* Mr. Cohen, please send me back my check. I'm sending you a *smaller* one: the balance I'm giving to them!

COHEN. My God, why are you shouting? Don't get so *emotional.*

SEYMOUR. What do you mean, don't get emotional? Jews get emotional. *(Points at COHEN.)* He works for the

United Jewish Appeal and he doesn't even know Jews are emotional!

COHEN. May I have a glass of water, Mrs. Goldstein?

SEYMOUR. Have whatever you want, but then please go!

COHEN. You begrudge me a little water?

SEYMOUR. Not at all! Give him a *full* glass! *(JOYCE gets water.)*

COHEN. *(placatingly)* ...Why are we fighting like this? This isn't you. This isn't me. They make people crazy. You're a businessman. Whatever you gave already is fine! All right, it's a little less than we expected, especially since your father-in-law's chairm...

SEYMOUR. One thousand to you! Fifteen hundred to *them.*

COHEN. *Fifteen hundred* to them??

SEYMOUR. That's right! For bail!

COHEN. *(eyes screw-up)* If you do that, I'll recommend they take your name off our letterhead.

SEYMOUR. You wouldn't do that.

COHEN. Oh, no? And no more bulletins *either!* *(He scoops up his briefcase, heads to door.)* Good-bye! And Norman Lear, the Communist, can drop dead altogether! *(He slams out.)*

SEYMOUR. Jeez, that Cohen. I don't know, he rubs me the wrong way.

JOYCE. Since when? You've known him for years!

(The doorbell rings. JOYCE answers it. It's MR. COHEN.)

COHEN. *(sheepish)* I left my newsletter. *(He goes to the couch, picks up newsletter, then turns to SEYMOUR and JOYCE.)* Look, since I'm back, can't we calmly sit down and talk this over?

SEYMOUR. I don't want to discuss anything, Mr. Cohen!

COHEN. *(An accusation, points to glass of water.)* You won't even let me finish my water? *(SEYMOUR turns away in aggravated frustration. MR. COHEN accepts this as permission, although begrudging, to drink the water. But almost automatically his arm holding the Federation's newsletter, rises up as if it had a life of its own and he suddenly starts reading at SEYMOUR:)* "We caution you not to be *deceived* by JDL suggestions that before their entrance into the scene, American Jewry was either indifferent or insensitive to the plight of Soviet Jewry!"

SEYMOUR. Five hundred dollars to *you* — Two thousand to *them!* *(SEYMOUR jams the briefcase under the U.J.A. man's arm and crowds him toward the door.)*

COHEN. *(shocked)* You're pushing me!?

SEYMOUR. I'm not pushing. I'm leading! *You're* pushing!

COHEN. Is this any way for a nice Jewish boy to act?!!

SEYMOUR. I am not a nice Jewish boy! *(SEYMOUR flings the door open. MR. COHEN is gone. SEYMOUR shuts the door hard. Then he turns, prowls around absently, drinks COHEN's water, then sits down heavily on the couch.)* Jeez, did I push him out?

JOYCE. Uh, I hope not, but I think so. It was hard to figure out there, it got jumbled.

SEYMOUR. Oh God, I shouldn't of done that! Why'd I do that?

JOYCE. And you finished his water too.

SEYMOUR. Boy, I'm glad he didn't see *that*. *(wry)* I'd be off the mailing list altogether.

JOYCE. Seymour, you can't really give them two thousand dollars?

SEYMOUR. When they called me *Seymour*, it had a certain feel, like a real name. Not a joke.

JOYCE. Seymour, I'm against it. It's my money too! *(He looks at her, then sighs deeply.)* And please, don't sigh, Seymour! *(She heads quickly into the kitchen, SEYMOUR following her.)*

(The stage is empty an instant... Then KEITH enters, carrying his tote bag, checks to see if anyone's there, then heads to the waste basket, fishes out the Nazi Rally leaflet. [The large black swastika is transparent from the back.] reads it, then compares it with a leaflet he pulls out of his back pocket. It's not the same. He slips it back in his pocket, then refolds the Nazi Rally leaflet and carefully places it back in the basket. He picks up his tote bag and heads toward front door, then, impulsively hesitates, turns the bag around where we see now K. GOLDSTEIN velcroed on his bag; with one quick tear he strips it off, then continues to door and exits. The curtain falls quickly.)

END OF SCENE I

Scene 2

TIME: 3:00 A.M. Sunday morning.

AT RISE: The set is dark, moonlight shining through the window. We hear night birds, a lone car passing by. The night is very quiet. SEYMOUR, dressed in pajamas and slippers, slowly comes down the stairs into the living room. He sighs deeply.

JOYCE. *(coming down the stairs)* Oh, God. Seymour. Please.

SEYMOUR. I thought you were asleep.

JOYCE. Yeah. Sure. You thought I was asleep.

SEYMOUR. I had a dream.

JOYCE. Can't we go to bed?

SEYMOUR. Sure, go ahead. I'm not stopping you. *(pause)* I can't sleep.

JOYCE. Are you really going to give them so much money?

SEYMOUR. I'm going to sleep.

JOYCE. Seymour.

SEYMOUR. You have your account. I have my account. That's the way you wanted it. Fine.

JOYCE. *(Lights a cigarette.)* Fine. You have a perfect right to give it to anyone you want.

SEYMOUR. You're lying.

JOYCE. That's-right.

SEYMOUR. Good-night... *(He takes a step toward stairs.)*

JOYCE. ...If you give them money, you're supporting what they do. Bombing Russian Embassy cars, fighting the PLO in the streets.

SEYMOUR. They don't do that anymore.

JOYCE. Yeah, so they say; but they did it.

SEYMOUR. You know the Russians'd never let *one* Jew out, if the JDL hadn't done something, something outrageous.

JOYCE. Don't apologize for them.

SEYMOUR. Hanging banners from a couple of synagogues, "Save Soviet Jewry," *That's* gonna move the Russians?? *(JOYCE crushes out her cigarette. She fluffs up pillows on the couch and sits.)* You know, Christians must be sick and tired of hearing us and our complaints. We're so sensitive, we don't let them live. They hear too much about us, our problems; if anything lasts too long, it's bound to irritate and anger people. What to say to the Jew and what *not* to say to the Jew to avoid hurting him. What a pain in the ass that must be...

JOYCE. Shhh ... Don't let the Christians hear... *(SEYMOUR laughs. He deflates himself into a chair. Then, no sooner than he does, he jack-knives up.)* What? What?

SEYMOUR. Nothing. *(He crosses, comes back.)* ...Guess who was a nice Jewish boy? Who never got into trouble in school? Never. Who was afraid of the teachers, the cops, the Christian kids; *and,* if you got in trouble, your *mother* had to come to school. And I *hated* that because Momma was so European .. no, not European — Jewish, no, not Jewish, *Yiddish,* her accent, her everything ... I was ashamed. Ashamed she was too Jewish. My God, is anyone ever too, too ... Chicano, too Black, too Vietnamese?

JOYCE. Where's the valium? *(She goes to her purse which is on the bar.)*

SEYMOUR. You're *totally* assimilated, and you're worried *you're* too Jewish.

JOYCE. I wouldn't mind being a White Anglo Saxon Protestant a while. But every time I come close, some lunatic bombs a synagogue in San Francisco.

SEYMOUR. "Sha! Seymour, Sha," she would say. "Quiet. Don't make trouble. Sha." She drummed this into my head, and into my brother Jacob's head ... *Layf avec, layf avec,* my mother always told me, and we ran away, all right. You heard of the Boston Marathon? I've trained for it all my life. I'm forty-five, and I still feel like a boy, a nice Jewish boy. You know what a nice Jewish boy is? Somebody who's scared all the time.

JOYCE. ... Are you telling this to your therapist?

SEYMOUR. I don't tell Silverman anything! He's a schmuck, too.

JOYCE. Then you shouldn't go, you're wasting money.

SEYMOUR. You told me to, I was getting on your nerves sighing. I sighed *maybe* once a week.

JOYCE. You were sighing all the time, Seymour. It can drive a person nuts.

SEYMOUR. Do you know Silverman told me he goes to a psychiatrist because *he's* scared of everything?

JOYCE. Seymour, this is ridiculous. You go to a psychiatrist, and he tells you *his* problems?

SEYMOUR. Yeah, it irritates me, him sharing my neurosis. *(grumbles)* The man's co-opting my neurosis. *(He crosses downstage right, sighs.)*

JOYCE. Please, Seymour, don't sigh.

SEYMOUR. I am not sighing. *(He gestures okay, okay, I forgot.)* You know, I got reminded of Mendl Splutkin... I haven't thought of him in years... *(remembers)* What a name. The only kid at P.S. 80 who'd fight the Irish. And the Italians too. *(Muses the name out loud with respect.)* Mendl Splutkin. Boy, could he fight... *(then a little depreciating)* Of course, Mendl ended up a cab driver, still in the Bronx. He's been robbed three times somebody told me. He never got anywhere. *(an impressed, long-ago memory)* You know, once in the school yard, a couple of Irish, they were tough, thrown out of Catholic School, St. Brendan's, and they were pushing me around. Hey, kike! ... I tried running away but they caught me, they wouldn't let me go, but Mendl saw it, some other Jewish kids did too but they ... they made believe they didn't see anything. But Mendl didn't make believe. He yelled, leave him alone, at *two* guys. Both bigger than him. One said, "fuck you, Jew bastard." And Mendl hit him. I mean Mendl hit him! I'll never forget the surprise on Tutty McGraw's face. But the other bastard, Boyce, hit Mendl, then jumped him, threw him down on the concrete. That was hard concrete. Not like the concrete today. But Mendl was fighting them both. *(admiringly)* Boy, that fucking Mendl. *(pause)* But I didn't do anything. Jesus, I was so scared I peed in my pants. I stood in the schoolyard like a schmuck, wet. My face got red hot; it was really burning.

Would you believe I still remember my hot face sometimes, and that's thirty years ago and Mendl fought them!

JOYCE. You talk as if *he* were the only one that ever fought them.

SEYMOUR. Yeah! Well, who else?!

JOYCE. Don't be ridiculous.

SEYMOUR. Who else??!

JOYCE. Ben-Gurion, that's who!

SEYMOUR. Yeah, but I never knew Ben-Gurion. I knew *Mendl.* Ben-Gurion didn't fight in the schoolyard.

JOYCE. Seymour, take a valium.

SEYMOUR. That Mendl. I let him cheat from me on tests after that. *(simply)* I loved Mendl. I tried teaching him Algebra. He just couldn't do it. God, I wish I could've taught him Algebra. *(shrugs)* But he was no dope ... Maybe he *owns* his own cab ... Uh, I think somebody told me he owns his own cab. *Yeah.* He owns his own cab. Do you know what a medallion costs in New York City? Plenty! *(a sudden burst of rueful anger)* Where the hell did he come off having guts with a name like *Mendl Splutkin!*

JOYCE. Seymour, forgive me, but that's a lot of worn-out macho stuff anyway. You're just not that type. Neither is your son.

SEYMOUR. Certainly I'm not that type ... What do you mean, I'm not that type?

JOYCE. You're educated, sensitive, more conscious; uh, you don't watch Monday Night Football.

SEYMOUR. Because I teach at U.C.L.A. that night!

JOYCE. My God, you've still got macho feelings. Not after that Macho Detox Program?

SEYMOUR. I didn't need that program. When did I have a macho feeling? I'm still waiting for the first one.

JOYCE. Would you really watch football if you didn't teach that night?

SEYMOUR. Yes! Maybe! ... No. I hate football! I always got hurt when I played football. *(wryly)* You know who never got hurt? Mendl!

JOYCE. *(Puts out her cigarette, throws a cursory glance at the mirror. At what she sees.)* Oh, God ... Seymour, please, let me get some sleep... *(She heads to stairs.)*

SEYMOUR. You want to hear my dream?

JOYCE. Tomorrow, it's four a.m., please.

SEYMOUR. It's their rally today.

JOYCE. Yeah, and if they wouldn't't've brought it up, you wouldn't't've known.

SEYMOUR. Yeah ... That's true.

JOYCE. And that would've been that.

SEYMOUR. *(He nods.)* Umm. *(pause)* You don't want to listen to my dream?

JOYCE. Uh-huh. *(JOYCE drags herself up the stairs and disappears. SEYMOUR lingers a second at the foot of stairs. JOYCE senses his disappointment. Pause.)* ...Is it a happy dream?

SEYMOUR. You'll love it.

JOYCE. The world's asleep, and I'm listening to dreams. Okay. *(She reappears, sits herself on stairs.)*

SEYMOUR. Okay ... I dreamt that I was middle-weight champion of the world. You know what kind of fists I had? Iron! I mean, my fists were made of *real* iron, it was a dream. I fought the light-heavyweight champ and destroyed him. Then the heavyweight champion and I gave him a shot, with the iron fist, he was down, a knock-out, what a shot, and I was the new *Heavyweight champion of the world!* .. of course, in the dream I was Black.

JOYCE. So that's what it was.

SEYMOUR. Was I tossing in my sleep? Hey, they were tough fights.

JOYCE. No. You were *sighing* in your sleep. Loud! *You* were having a wonderful dream, and I'm up all night. *(not without affection)* As your brother would say, oi marriage.

SEYMOUR. *(He walks over to the window, turns back to JOYCE)* ... My father took me for a walk on Bainbridge and 204th, that was a nice thing he used to do. I'm going to do it with Keith, it's not too late ... It was after the war, some new Nazi outfit. They were having a meeting outside the bank — just one block from a Jewish neighborhood. What chutzpah; the contempt, an anti-Semitic meeting right in a Jewish neighborhood. We passed by, it was an accident, we were going down to the Parkway. I asked my father how could they say such things about us, why didn't somebody do something? He pulled me away hard, "Quiet, am I crazy?" and dragged me away. Even if he'd just yelled "Bullshit," or "Drop dead, fascists," or ... or even "Al Jolson," anything, then run ... I know it's unfair, I know it's irrational, but ... all these years later, I didn't cry at my father's funeral ... I liked the man, but I was surprised that I didn't, it shook me up. I didn't tell you about it; but I *thought* I'd cry. I wanted to cry... *(anguishing)* It couldn't've been just that one incident, could it...?

JOYCE. *This* you *gotta* talk to your therapist about.

SEYMOUR. I did, I did. Silverman said, "You were tremendously outnumbered." and I said, "But it was right near a Jewish neighborhood. We outnumbered them ten to one!" So he said, "Listen, they don't do that kind of thing here any more," and I said, "Skokie" and he said, "Your hour's up for today."

JOYCE. *(She sighs.)* He probably wants a Korean wife too.

SEYMOUR. Japanese. Silverman's wife's Japanese. But he's got marital problems anyhow, thank God. I don't know why that made me so happy.

JOYCE. Bellow, Joe Heller, Phillip Roth, sure, everybody blames Jewish women for everything ... Listen, Seymour, the Med-Fly was not our fault. *(She sighs.)*

SEYMOUR. *(dry)* Joyce. Please. Don't sigh. *(Steps away, turns back to his wife.)* I was walking to French Charlie's to play pick-up baseball with three or four other kids; we passed a porch with four boys on it, and they yelled the old shit and we froze, all except *Mendl*. Two at a time, he was up those stairs. Zap, he punched one guy over the railing, socked another, threw another guy down and the other ran. And you know something? Later, they became Mendl's friends! *His friends.* Not right away, but later! I couldn't believe it. God, how I loved that Mendl. *(just recalling)* But you know something? I just remember, I was just about to go up those steps myself, but it was all so quick... *(very pleased)* Yeah, that's right. That's true. I'm glad I remembered that. It's about time I remembered something good about myself.

JOYCE. You sure Mendl wasn't jush rash? Don't confuse courage with rashness. Sometimes what masquerades as courage may turn out to be simply bravado, used to compensate for one's unconscious fear and prove one's machismo.

SEYMOUR. ...How much longer is your Encounter Session?

JOYCE. They just made it into a Marathon,

SEYMOUR. A marathon. Terrific.

JOYCE. *(drowsily)* Seymour, I gotta go to sleep. *(She looks at herself in mirror.)* God, I look terrible. *(She drags herself up the stairs.)*

SEYMOUR. *(There's a deep silence. Calling up the stairs.)* Today's their rally... Joyce. *(No answer; she's asleep.)* Joyce? *(He goes to window. Looks out a crack, but does not pull the curtain, turns away, walks about without direction in the room, then crosses to the bar... and the waste basket. He fishes in and draws out something. The Nazi Party rally leaflet. He looks straight ahead a second. Then he walks slowly to the living room window. He pulls the curtains. The light from the false dawn is just appearing. SEYMOUR looks at the leaflet once more... and then stares out the window where dawn gets brighter and brighter. The curtain slowly comes down on the new day.)*

END OF ACT I

ACT TWO

TIME: 9 A.M., Sunday morning.

AT RISE: SEYMOUR, at a chinning bar, newly placed between the jambs of the door leading off stage right. He looks at it, almost malevolently. Then hunches, readies himself to spring up — he sucks in a deep breath, jumps up and grabs bar, tries to do one pull-up ... he struggles up ... barely makes one. He fights for two but it is in vain; he can't make it. He slumps down, omits a deep, aggravated sigh at his inability. Antsy, he walks away. JOYCE, dressed in simple morning dress, has come in.

JOYCE. What are you doing that for now? *(slight pause)* How many did you do?

SEYMOUR. I don't know. Five or six.

JOYCE. How many??

SEYMOUR. One.

JOYCE. You should've taken a Valium last night.

SEYMOUR. I could've done more. When you're nervous, you're tense, and what happens when you're tense? Oxygen stops or something, who the hell knows, leave me alone, Joyce.

JOYCE. Sure, that's what I do best, leaving people alone ... Let's go to the Marina for brunch.

SEYMOUR. It's too early for brunch.

JOYCE. By the time we go, by the time we get there.
SEYMOUR. Where's Keith?
JOYCE. I drove him to the "Y".
SEYMOUR. For God's sake, it's only ten blocks, downhill. Why couldn't he walk?
JOYCE. I don't know, I drive him everywhere, it's a habit. Look, didn't we want those deck chairs? K-Mart's got a sale. Today only.
SEYMOUR. You took 'im an hour early.
JOYCE. Hey, we'll brunch in the Marina. Then go to K-Mart.
SEYMOUR. I want out of the house, too, Joyce.
JOYCE. You said I outgrew K-Mart. Come on, I'll show you.
SEYMOUR. We protect Keith from everything.
JOYCE. I don't want to run into them, let's go.
SEYMOUR. His life is filtered.
JOYCE. Please don't start, no instant summary of our life. Leave Keith alone.
SEYMOUR. I'm not starting. He never plays in the street.
JOYCE. What street? We live in the hills. There are no kids here. There are no *streets* here.
SEYMOUR. Then why the hell did we buy here?
JOYCE. Because the hills are where people live who are "with it." You wanted big accounts? We don't do coke, we don't wear cowboy boots, we don't drive a Mercedes, at least we can live in the hills.
SEYMOUR. That's not the only reason.
JOYCE. Please!
SEYMOUR. Okay, I'm just saying.

JOYCE. It was your idea, too. I didn't need Beverly Hills. I could've lived in Malibu.

SEYMOUR. It was your idea, after Keith's school became black.

JOYCE. You agreed.

SEYMOUR. I don't know ... I'm his father. Maybe I should've taught him to work it out. Not move. *There* he never got punched. We send him to *private* school, he gets punched.

JOYCE. All right!

SEYMOUR. We always move. The Italians don't move. The Irish don't move, *We* move. *(JOYCE quickly drops in two ... then a third Alka Seltzer in a glass of water, drinks.)* Save me some. *(He sighs deeply.)*

JOYCE. Don't sigh, Seymour. *Please* don't sigh.

SEYMOUR. I mean, the boy's sheltered. He stays in the house too much. I mean, we've taken the struggle away from him. We don't even let him take the bus.

JOYCE. The buses aren't safe.

SEYMOUR. Joyce, he may have to take the bus some day.

JOYCE. Seymour, this is not the Bronx. When you grew up there were dozens of kids running around, a million things to do, a street life. People walked. It's Blacks and Puerto Ricans and old people now. Why do you think everyone ran to the suburbs? For the greenery? Get used to it, and leave me alone with it.

SEYMOUR. But shouldn't he know a *little* of what real life is?

JOYCE. We moved to Beverly Hills to get away from real life.

SEYMOUR. I know, but a person should know how to ride a bus.

JOYCE. Why?

SEYMOUR. I mean, what are you talking about, what if he has to ride a bus?

JOYCE. Why? We'll buy him a car.

SEYMOUR. *(some answer)* We'll buy him a car. Okay, till then?

JOYCE. I'll drive him.

SEYMOUR. You're not a chauffeur. He's got to learn to cope.

JOYCE. *(flaring)* What do you want? Him punched in the mouth again?

SEYMOUR. That kid was younger and smaller!

JOYCE. Then you should have taught him to fight back!

SEYMOUR. I know!

JOYCE. Take him to karate again.

SEYMOUR. *(Walks away.)* I don't know, we came from *neighborhoods,* all kinds of people, It was natural okay competition in the streets. You had great pals, you explored together, you played in the schoolyard, you didn't call on the phone to see them; and for our kids we made vanilla and bland and they watch TV; at least we learned to cope with a few things, we were the agents of our own development a little, and nobody drove us every place.

JOYCE. You want street life? Move to Venice and get shot! Your Bronx is dead, will you get that through your head? The neighborhood's gone; okay, you played in the street and hung out at the corner candy store. Gone! Gone with the radio programs and the egg cream. The telephone replaced the stoop. And when they could, *everybody* escaped. Well, we all escaped but into God alone knows what. Vacuous land; dullsville. To buy a container of milk I drive two miles! Nobody knows anybody here, everybody's strangers. That's what we made, that's what we have, and even with your big deal Bronx you became what you became, so let's go to brunch, K-Mart and then a movie. A comedy!

SEYMOUR. You sent Keith away, insulate him from what's going down today, right?

JOYCE. Why? Is this good for him? *(She fishes in her dress pocket and whips out a leaflet, shakes it at him.)* You left it on the dresser. *(She tears the leaflet in a dozen pieces and flings it at the waste basket.)*

SEYMOUR. He should know.

JOYCE. *(almost drops her voice)* He knows enough! *Seymour,* sometimes I don't even want Keith studying our history. Look at it — crowded with ghosts of Roman Legionnaires, Inquisitors, Cossacks, Storm Troopers, P.L.O., talk about a collective unconscious. And Simon Weisenthal gives me a pain in the ass, I know that's sacrilegious but God, I wish he'd retire already and marry a *shiksa.*

SEYMOUR. I didn't invite the Nazi convention to L.A. They came by themselves. You can't sanforize history or life, Joyce. Someday people have to take a *bus*. He's going to hear about it sooner or later, at school, in the street, on TV. Somebody's going to spring it on him again and shouldn't he be a little fortified by something, at least knowledge? He's got to know how to handle it. He can't hide in the closet.

JOYCE. Why can't we hide in the closet. Just once?! *(And suddenly, on a mad impulse, she turns abruptly and walks into the closet and shuts the door behind her.)*

SEYMOUR. *(at the door)* Joyce! Come out of there!

JOYCE. No!

SEYMOUR. What are you doing? *Joyce.*

(There's no response. He tugs on the handle, but she fights him from the other side. They are unaware that KEITH, tote bag in hand, has appeared in the doorway and is watching.)

SEYMOUR. Joyce, what the hell are you doing, come out of there!

JOYCE. *(She comes out sheepishly and in answer to his look: Small shrug.)* I just felt like it. I don't know what happened.

SEYMOUR. Was it nice in there...? *(JOYCE nods dolefully. They turn as KEITH, with an askance look, enters the room.)*

KEITH. What were you doing in there, Mom?

JOYCE. Uh, I was looking for, uh, a sweater, not really, it's too hard to explain. *(KEITH heads up the stairs to his room.)*

SEYMOUR. You walked home?

KEITH. David's Mom drove me. *(exits)*

SEYMOUR. Oh. *(That irritates him, and to hide it, he exits into kitchen.)*

JOYCE. *(Alone, she checks out the chinning bar and, without thinking, grabs the bar, does two quick chin-ups ... hangs there ... then does a quick third, drops to her feet.)* Huh. *(She shies away from the bar as KEITH comes down the stairs.)*

KEITH. Mom.

JOYCE. Yes, Keith.

KEITH. Ahh ... you busy?

JOYCE. Yes! No. What?

KEITH. Some kids were talking.

JOYCE. Yes, Keith, what? *(Calls out to kitchen.)* Don't eat anything, Seymour, we're going to the Marina.

KEITH. What's "Never Again"?

JOYCE. Oh, God. *(She strides to her cigarettes, lights one.)* You should ask your father.

KEITH. Uh, That's O.K.

JOYCE. He's in the kitchen.

KEITH. What does it mean?

JOYCE. Seymour!

KEITH. Let him alone, Mom. Forget it.

SEYMOUR. *(O.S.)* What? *(the slightest beat as mother and son look at each other)*

JOYCE. Nothing ... *(Drops her voice.)* Keith, you're going to have to talk to your father.

KEITH. "Never Again," Mom.

JOYCE. I think it means the Jews will fight back next time, which there won't be.

KEITH. At school, we...

JOYCE. He was bigger than you!

KEITH. Come on, Mom.

JOYCE. We intend taking precautions from allowing it to happen again. That's why I suppose there's a Jewish Defense League.

KEITH. I thought you were against them.

JOYCE. I am against them. Keith, please. Get a jacket, we're going to the Marina. *(KEITH exits.)*

(SEYMOUR has entered.)

SEYMOUR. Did you hear what you just said?
JOYCE. I panicked.
SEYMOUR. That's the J.D.L.'s official party line.
JOYCE. *(rubbing her headachy temple)* I know. I know.
SEYMOUR. You wanna go back in the closet?
JOYCE. Yes! *(She strides into the closet.)*
SEYMOUR. *(He follows, stands at closed door, shrugs.)* What the hell. *(Goes into closet, closes door. From inside closet:)* I feel foolish saying this, but to me this is better than Club Med.
JOYCE. Me, too.

(The doorbell rings.)

SEYMOUR. *(jumpy)* It's them.
JOYCE. *(sotto voce)* Don't answer it.
SEYMOUR. Uh .. our cars are in the driveway.
JOYCE. *(The closet door opens tentatively and JOYCE crosses to door, answers, relaxes, speaks sharply.)* What do you want?
JERRY. *(offstage)* Is that any way to speak to a brother-in-law? *(JERRY enters in an up party mood.)* C'mon, gang. I'll take you kids to breakfast.
SEYMOUR. We're going to brunch, then to K-Mart.
JERRY. You wake me up to talk about Mendl, and now you don't want to go to breakfast? *(to JOYCE)* They were going to throw Seymour out of school, all A's and out, because he let that dope Mendl cheat from him on tests. *(deprecatingly)* He's a cab driver now.
SEYMOUR. He *owns* his *own* cab, Jacob, goddamnit!

JERRY. I told you a million times *Jerry*. Not Jacob. And he's a cab driver.

SEYMOUR. He's not.

JOYCE. We have to go, Seymour. *(She exits.)*

JERRY. What did you do to the U.J.A. man, Cohen?

SEYMOUR. Nothing.

JERRY. Don't tell me nothing. Cohen says you grabbed his briefcase, you pushed him out, you refused him a glass of water.

SEYMOUR. Ask Joyce. We gave him a full glass.

JERRY. He said he had to leave some.

SEYMOUR. And you believed him.

JERRY. How many times have you invited me for dinner?

SEYMOUR. Oh, Christ, don't start with that.

JERRY. A man who doesn't invite his own brother for dinner? Of course I believe Cohen.

SEYMOUR. We didn't invite you that much because we couldn't get along with your ex.

JERRY. So what. I couldn't get along with her either, but I still ate dinner with her every night.

SEYMOUR. Now we can't get along with *you.*

JERRY. Why? Why can't you get along with me? Because I think you're ridiculous? — Busting my chops lately about Mendl. I want to forget all that shit. That's why I came to California. They're interested in suntans here and acupuncture facelifts here and aerobics here, and they're *smart.* Being Jewish is a misfortune, a burden, a pain in the ass, and I don't want it. I don't identify with it. With me it's an historical accident, and I don't want it. My first wife was Gentile, my second wife was Philippino

Catholic and Uncle Morris was right. Now I'm thinking of *Korean* women. They don't know from Jews. It'll take them a while yet to be anti-Semitic. Is it any wonder that Disraeli, Heinrich Heine and Bob Dylan converted? They didn't want the aggravation and I'll tell you something — if they could have found Korean wives on Olympic Boulevard, they would have married Koreans, too.

SEYMOUR. Who didn't want to leave last Passover's Seder? Who went around the table kissing everyone, shouting he doesn't care what anyone says, Manischevitz is the best California Red? Who put horseradish on sponge cake? and said it was like a cherry sundae? ... Who collected all the matzoh crumbs in a paper bag and whispered it was the flakes of Heaven, who? .. Who didn't want to leave last Passover and stayed up all night and stared out the window? .. Who?

JERRY. I told you, I'm trying to stop drinking.

SEYMOUR. *(pointing)* The man's ashamed of his identity and obsessed with it. Why didn't the Jews defend themselves in Germany, Poland, the death camps!?

JERRY. *(Throws his hands up in the air; this subject drives him up the wall.)* Oh, my God, for Christ's sake, not again. You're starting again. They were outnumbered, Seymour. They couldn't forsee the ferocity of the Nazis, they were disorganized, scared, a demoralized people living in an increasingly hostile environment.

SEYMOUR. Where'd you get that?

JERRY. I *read* it. I read it in a fat book and *memorized* it so I could answer you back. *(Pantomimes an arrow entering his chest.)* Gotcha.

SEYMOUR. I don't want to get into that argument—

JERRY. Mazeltov!

SEYMOUR. — but they were natural victims. They gave the sanction of the victims. They walked into the ovens like sheep. Doesn't that bother you?

JERRY. No, it doesn't bother me! Certainly it bothers me. Leave me alone. That's forty years ago. It's ancient history.

SEYMOUR. I don't know why this is but somehow .. I feel .. I've lost face .. I'm a little ashamed of it...

JERRY. You've lost face?? What are you, a Samurai? What is this, "Shogun"? That's what comes from associating with fanatics. Just their presence jangles people. They feed on that anxiety.

SEYMOUR. You think I need them to make me anxious? I'm riveted *together* by anxieties. I wake up every morning anxious, something's going to happen to me. Something's going to happen to Joyce, to Keith, to the business, Israel, America. They suddenly leap up in my mind for no reason. I can't go on a vacation without being afraid that the minute I walk in, the hotel's cancelling my reservations.

JERRY. How come you're not afraid something's going to happen to *me?* I'm your brother.

SEYMOUR. All right, you too.

JERRY. I'm an afterthought. I've had one massive heart attack, did you forget that? You forgot that, didn't you?

SEYMOUR. I took you to the hospital. It was indigestion! *All right. All right.* I said you too.

JERRY. *(He emits a semi-satisfied grunt.)* But when I was lying there in the hospital, you didn't bring me Gatorade when I asked you.

SEYMOUR. I did! Your wife drank it!

JERRY. She drank my Gatorade?.. Why not. She got the house, she got the car, she got the Gatorade!

SEYMOUR. I won't go sixty miles an hour, not because of the speed limit, but because I worry that the minute I get in the car, air is leaking out of the tires.

(JOYCE enters, She's changed clothes and is dressed to go to the Marina.)

JOYCE. He does *forty* in the *fast* lane. People honk, they go berserk. Seymour, let's go.

SEYMOUR. When I was with them, for a second I wasn't afraid. They don't cry and kvetch and moan and look for sympathy and try to be nice guys and keep a low profile or any of that garbage — which you can't do anyway if the shit hits the fan. They say: Leave us alone; stop firing Katyusha rockets at us. If you hurt us, we're not going to hold a big meeting to discuss the root causes of anti-Semitism, we're going to knock your fucking brains out!

JERRY. *(watching his brother's manner carefully)* Uh-oh, we got trouble here.

SEYMOUR. *(Suddenly starts stalking about the living room, in and about furniture, the TV, the lamps, abruptly picks up a throw pillow, flings it back on couch. They stare at him; he turns back to them.)* I'm going down to the Republic.

JOYCE. Oh, my God! He's losing his mind!

JERRY. Are you nuts? Ohrbach's is one of your biggest clients. JDL *picketed Ohrbach's* over carrying Russian goods.

SEYMOUR. Uh .. Police'll keep us apart .. I hope. No one'll know I'm there.

JERRY. Moses from Mt. Sinai, and I don't mean the hospital, just spoke to me, via satellite, you know what he said? You're a schmuck. You got national clients. What if you get arrested? It gets on TV? You'll be out of business. You'll have to work for me again. I'll start you off as a *bookkeeper*.

JOYCE. Seymour, you're an important businessman in the community. C'mon. These JDL people are misfits, unemployed kooks, *nobodies*.

SEYMOUR. There's a well-known screenwriter goes with them all the time!

JERRY. I know, I know, quiet, shh, take it easy. I heard about that guy from a client. He's nuts. They reject his scripts, so he wants to fight somebody. *Anybody*. That's the kind of people they attract. Seymour, you have a Master's Degree, Harvard School of Business.

SEYMOUR. They're knocking over gravestones again!

JERRY. A few cranks. They were kids, a gang initiation. They picked at random.

SEYMOUR. There was a Catholic cemetery right next door, Jacob.

JERRY. Listen to me. People like you demonstrate for Blacks, against Vietnam, for E.R.A., Save the Whales, not, not ... *this*. This, this is not respectable. You live in Beverly Hills.

SEYMOUR. Listen, I'm not nine years old, you're my older brother, but not forever.

JERRY. *(Throws up his hands.)* You want a mid-life crisis, go ahead, have a mid-life crisis. Other men abandon their families, change jobs, run after young girls, but no, my brother wants to go fight Nazis!

JOYCE. I don't want you going down there, please, even to protest, Seymour.

SEYMOUR. I'm forty-five years old, and she's forbidding me to go someplace. *(He crosses quickly to bedroom and exits.)*

JOYCE. *(Follows him.)* Look. Look. We've built something comfortable here. Something pleasant. I like it, Keith likes it. If *they* hadn't showed up here, you wouldn't even have known about downtown. *(SEYMOUR comes back in toting a pair of very old cracked GI combat boots.)* What's that?

SEYMOUR. My old army boots. *(He sits, starts to blow dust off boots but before she can say anything, he whips some newspapers from the couch.)* I bought paper, I brought paper. *(He spreads papers on floor, places boots on them.)*

JOYCE. You haven't worn those in twenty years. They won't fit. Feet grow.

SEYMOUR. Feet don't grow. I got out of the army at twenty-four. My feet are still the same size feet.

JOYCE. Feet get bigger. You're going to a doctor. Ask him.

SEYMOUR. You think I'm going to ask Silverman if my feet are growing? — absolutely not.

JOYCE. Not only bigger. Wider too.

SEYMOUR. All right, Joyce, all right. I'm sorry about this. I'm not going against you, but I said I'm going. *(JERRY has sat quietly, taking a spectator's seat.)*

JOYCE. *(ticked off)* Where are you going? What will you fight with? You don't have a muscle in your entire body.

JERRY. Oi marriage.

SEYMOUR. *(Turns on JERRY.)* Why don't you get out of here!

JERRY. Why? I'm enjoying it. Why should you two still be married when everybody else is divorced?

SEYMOUR. You're serious about that, aren't you?

JERRY. I'm only kidding, I'm only kidding. Go on, fight. Doctors say it's healthy. Look how fighting helped my three marriages. *(He exits to kitchen.)*

JOYCE. Those guys, they were here, you saw, kids, agile, in their twenties, *kids*. Nobody your age. Six months ago you tried climbing the wall out back, you were a great climber in the Bronx you said; you fell down, you scraped your shin, right away you shouted, "Gangrene, Cedars-Sinai Emergency will be closed."

SEYMOUR. That movie writer goes. He's my age. I bet he couldn't climb that goddamned wall either!

JOYCE. He's a failure, like everybody connected with them. You think Neil Simon goes into the streets with them? He's writing, making money, taking care of business. The J.D.L., they're people who don't have anything to lose. You saw, roughnecks, unstable thugs.

SEYMOUR. Who did you want to go face Nazis? Yeshiva boys with long payesses, and pale faces? Who? The front four of the Hadassah — with a blue rinse? Who?

JOYCE. You can't go fight Nazis every time they show in the street. I know they seem high profile now, I know they're getting press. My head's not in the sand — at least, not all the way — The human body carries bacteria, but it's not dangerous if the body's healthy. Okay, if there's psychological illness, or an economic depression, then maybe the bacteria could take over. I doubt it, the country's too fragmented. I just say let them evaporate, disappear. They will. They always have here, they'd probably go after the Blacks first anyway, you have no experience with violence. You're not a street fighter, for our sake, for Keith's sake... *(gesturing to boots)* ...throw those things away. *(SEYMOUR stares at his old army boots a beat. He takes a step away from them.)*

(JERRY enters from kitchen, nibbling on a piece of carrot.)

JERRY. Listen, let's go get some lox at this Korean deli, it's tasteless but at least it's not salty.

SEYMOUR. You and your Korean lox. You couldn't stand it if I went down there.

JERRY. Listen, don't start on me — fight with your wife.

SEYMOUR. Even in *this* you're competitive.

JERRY. Remember Uncle Abe's advice to his son Hymie, "Everything's a business, make money, and don't be ridiculous." You're my kid brother, you shouldn't be ridiculous.

SEYMOUR. You'd never go, but it'd be worse if I went. Somehow, *somehow,* that'd show you up.

JERRY. Listen. I don't want you doing something stupid and getting hurt. When they took your blood in the army, what happened?

SEYMOUR. I don't remember.

JERRY. Sey-mour.

SEYMOUR. I fainted.

JERRY. See? You always hated blood.

SEYMOUR. Yah. I see. Thanks for reminding me. *(Screws up his face.)* What's that all about?

JERRY. Don't be ridiculous.

SEYMOUR. I can't help it if I'm more succeful than you. It just happened. I didn't plan it that way. Consciously.

JERRY. I don't hold anything against you.. You're not more successful. *(Reconsiders in his own way.)* You got more money, you got a family, a wife, a son, a home, and you still feel something. *(a Jewish shrug)* But is that more successful?

JOYCE. Please understand my feelings. Keith's never run into this, not really. Don't bring it home. You love him; don't set him apart. Do you want him looking over his shoulder all his life, like you? *(SEYMOUR is very quiet.)* And me? Let's look away, a little benign neglect, please.

SEYMOUR. Well, Keith .. I was worked up before..

JOYCE. No, no, I respect you for wanting to do something, but this isn't it. All right, donate two thousand dollars. It kills me, but okay. But don't go. I'd be scared to death if you went.

SEYMOUR. I don't think the police can keep people apart.

JERRY. Seymour, you never had a fight in your life. You like physical pain? You hate physical pain. You're not coordinated, you'll stumble, you'll fall, you'll tear an Achilles tendon, it's murder.

SEYMOUR. Y-eah, I didn't think of that. An Achilles tendon .. uh, maybe I'll just send in a check.

JERRY. A torn Achilles tendon, surgery, with complications, the doctors always make complications. You think your insurance'll cover you? After they see the police report? Disqualified! Zap, there goes the summer house in Malibu.

JOYCE. No, we're buying in Trancas now.

JERRY. Trancas, Malibu, so what. The doctors'll get the beach house wherever it is.

SEYMOUR. An Achilles tendon.. well, I didn't say I was *definitely* going. Did I say I was definitely going? I'm just considering it. *(He moves further and further away from his old army boots. He eyes them from across the room.)*

JOYCE. You remember that Hollywood party? Somebody brought up the synagogue bombing in Idaho, but only the Christians would talk about it; you know how I knew that producer was Jewish? Because he immediately changed the subject. People don't want to be reminded. The J.D.L. reminds them. They talk too openly about being Jewish. The Jews cringe. They hate that, especially those that are passing, who want to disappear. Look at your brother here, with Koreans. You heard what he said before.

JERRY. That's not true. I'm proud of being a Jew, I just don't want to be Jewish... *(He heads to bathroom, leans into SEYMOUR, sotto voce.)* You want to fight downtown? *(Throws a significant glance toward JOYCE.)* You have enough trouble right here. *(JERRY exits.)*

SEYMOUR. *(Crosses to boots, picks them up and starts to exit to bedroom.)* I should've saddle-soaped them.

JOYCE. They're all cracked.

SEYMOUR. I'm throwing them out. *(He exits.)*

JOYCE. *(calling out)* Get a hat, let's take the convertible.

Keith, come on! We're going!

(JERRY enters.)

JERRY. Well, if you're going to brunch, which incidentally you didn't invite me... *(JOYCE picks up her handbag, looks in mirror, touches up her hair, heads toward door.)*

SEYMOUR. *(Enters, carrying sweater, follows her but slows down before he gets to door.)* Uh, listen, Joyce. *(She stops, her hand on doorknob, turns to him.)* At least I should be here, give them a check in person.

JOYCE. Seymour. Leave a note.

SEYMOUR. Didn't I wait in the cold with you for "Women Against Violence Against Women"?

JOYCE. That was safe. Just send them a check.

SEYMOUR. Joyce, didn't I wait while people made speeches against men?

JOYCE. They may never show up. We'll sit and wait like damn fools. *(She parks herself in an armchair, folds her arms in front of her. She's rigid. Then she drums her fingers loudly on the side table.)*

SEYMOUR. *(The sound jars his teeth, and he paces as far away from it as he can.)* Okay!

JOYCE. Okay! Fine! We'll just sit here!

SEYMOUR. *Fine!*

JOYCE. *FINE!* *(She crosses her arms again in a gesture of angry permanency, there's a tense silence. Then SEYMOUR cannot repress a deep, perhaps retaliatory sigh. JOYCE leaps up.)* That's it! I'm cleaning the house. *(She snatches the newspaper, crumples it violently.)*

SEYMOUR. The maid cleans the house.

JOYCE. Today I'm cleaning the house. *(She cleans silently, furiously. SEYMOUR eyes her, bristling. There's an electric silence as JOYCE "cleans". and SEYMOUR stands glaring at her. Suddenly, she stops cleaning.)* K-Mart'll close.

SEYMOUR. They're open 'till midnight.

JOYCE. I could go by myself, you know!

SEYMOUR. I just want to tell them in person. *(She flings down the crumpled newspaper, stalks off stage right. SEYMOUR stalks off stage left.)*

JERRY. *(He has followed first JOYCE with his head, then SEYMOUR. He turns slowly to audience, shakes his head.)* Oi, marriage .. And I'll probably do it again.

(JOYCE reenters trailing vacuum cleaner, plugs it in, vacuums. SEYMOUR reenters carrying a bottle of Lemon Pledge and a fistful of rags, cleans coffee table.)

JOYCE. *(Snaps off vacuum cleaner.)* Since when do you clean the house?

SEYMOUR. *Today I'M cleaning the house. See, Lemon fucking Pledge.*

(She snaps the machine back on. Suddenly, there's a loud rap on the back door made by a wooden cane. SEYMOUR crosses toward the back door, and UNCLE MORRIS bangs in.)

UNCLE MORRIS. Listen, what's going on?

SEYMOUR. Nothing, nothing.

UNCLE MORRIS. I know nothing. Why do you think I'm here? Where's my check?

SEYMOUR. You check? We gave you...

UNCLE MORRIS. My support, it's not in the mail.

JERRY. You gave it away to your ketzelles.

UNCLE MORRIS. I only give to the "Society to Cure Terrible Prostate Trouble."

(The doorbell rings, JOYCE goes to door, looks out peephole, turns back to SEYMOUR in room.)

JOYCE. It's them. *(Lowers her voice.)* I'm going to tell them you're not home.

SEYMOUR. *Joyce.*

(A beat. She opens the door reluctantly. JOE, SUSANA and DOUG enter.)

SUSANA. Morris!

UNCLE MORRIS. *(his arm outstretched)* Ketzella!

JERRY. *(thunderstruck)* She's your ketzella?

UNCLE MORRIS. *(He fishes around in his inside jacket pocket, finds something and presents JOE with support checks. Warmly gesturing to the three J.D.L ers)* They are all my ketzellas.

JERRY. My money's in the toilet.

JOE. *(Glances at checks.)* So, what's it gonna be, Seymour? You have to endorse 'em over, Morris.

UNCLE MORRIS. Why not? I have no wife, no children, no relatives. *(SEYMOUR and JERRY react badly at the news. UNCLE MORRIS quickly endorses checks.)*

DOUG. But you got widows, huh, Morris?

UNCLE MORRIS. *(devilish)* Widows I got ... I just wish they'd stop with the Percodan. *(Puts on his hat, hefts his cane.)* Okay, boys. Let's go to the Republic.

JOE. You're too old to go, Morris.

UNCLE MORRIS. Too old to go? I'm going. I ran away from the Jew haters in Russia, I ran away from them in Germany, I ran away from them in Jersey City. I'll be goddamned if I'll run away from them in Los Angeles, where you can't breathe from the smog. *(He shakes his cane angrily in air, taking support off his leg — he'd go down, but for the agile giant DOUG who steadies him.)*

SEYMOUR. If he's going, I'm going!

UNCLE MORRIS. What are you going to do there? You're a nebbish.

SEYMOUR. Stop saying that.

JOE. Come on, let's go. We got one more stop. We'll pick you up in ten minutes. *(to DOUG and SUSANA)* Let's go. *(They head to door.)*

SEYMOUR. *(Calls out.)* What should I bring?

JOE. Bring bail money. *(They exit.)*

SEYMOUR. Bring bail money.. *(scared)* Oh God.. *(regretting his decision already)* I just hope, I mean, even if I go, and there's trouble, that I don't run away.

UNCLE MORRIS. Well, Seymour, you know how you'll find out? *(talmudic)* If you run away, you'll know you ran away, and if you don't run away, you'll know you didn't run away. Once and for all, you'll know.

JERRY. You're senile.

UNCLE MORRIS. That's right ... but not every minute. *(MORRIS exits out back door. SEYMOUR heads into bedroom, returns carrying his army boots, parks himself on couch, puts boots on floor —* doesn't *put newspaper on floor this time. Starts unlacing his street shoes.)*

JOYCE. In North Carolina the Nazis had guns. *(SEYMOUR fights his way into first boot, stops a scared second.. then goes on, unloosens the laces, undoes a couple of eyes, stretches second boot.)* You go down there, I won't be here, Seymour. *(He looks at his wife.. She looks back at him. SEYMOUR inspects a crack in the boot.. Then SEYMOUR gets other boot on, stamps his feet into them, JOYCE turns abruptly, heads for bedroom.)* I can't find my keys. Where are my keys? I'm going to K-Mart! *(Exits to bedroom.)*

SEYMOUR. *(to JERRY)* Please! My wife and I are going to have a terrible fight. Go to your Swami Vuctananda. Let him turn the other cheek, he can afford it.

JERRY. What other cheek? He says punch 'em in the mouth.

SEYMOUR. Then come down. I'm scared to go alone.

JERRY. *He* says punch 'em in the mouth. *I* don't. He's my guru only for certain things.

SEYMOUR. What the hell do you think Nazis are? They're intellectual heirs of Hitler. Can't you get it through your head they mean what they say? If they can pull it off, they mean the ovens.

JERRY. Leave me alone, I don't want to hear that. Go — fight with your wife. *(He pushes his brother toward bedroom.)*

SEYMOUR. *(Grabs JERRY's arm.)* What the hell's wrong with us? I don't understand the Jews! A non-Jew goes outside, and he sees a dark cloud. He figures it's going to rain. He goes inside for an umbrella. Not a Jew. A Jew's got to catch pneumonia first. *(JERRY pulls away. SEYMOUR follows him.)* Self-defense is the first law of any living organism — if it doesn't adapt to that simple principle of nature, it doesn't deserve to go on.

JERRY. What self-defense? You're provoking them.

SEYMOUR. We have a right to counter-demonstrate.

JERRY. That's bullshit. Nobody'll control themselves. It's like two scorpions in a bottle.

SEYMOUR. It's honor, it's self-defense.

JERRY. Stop with the self-defense. Where do you know from self-defense?

SEYMOUR. *(a clash of thunder)* Don't do that, Jacob!

JERRY. All right. Okay. You're right. I've got to stop that. *(Rubs his temple, realizes what he's been doing.)* God. *(Distraught, he paces the room.)* I'm going to stop that, I promise. You know the biggest influence in my life? Not teachers or Elvis or college or John Kennedy. Adolph Hitler. It was *Adolph Hitler.* Remember those newsreels of the Nuremberg Rallies? They absolutely fascinated me. Hitler speaking, the violence, the rage — at *me.* God, I hated him, but I was morbidly fascinated too, isn't that terrible? — All at the same time. Talk about mixed up. Sometimes I believed I'd done something terrible, but what was it? I couldn't figure it out. Maybe I was guilty of something but *what?* Why do we always have to apologize for our existence? Why? Nobody else has to! Is it any wonder I'm crazed and demented?

SEYMOUR. You'd have been crazed and demented no matter what.

JERRY. That's true. *(He starts to kitchen.)* God, what happened to the Sixties? Everything was so quiet and peaceful then... *(He crosses into kitchen.)*

(SEYMOUR resumes lacing his boots. Suddenly, he is startled as UNCLE MORRIS enters from back door.)

SEYMOUR. I thought you went...

UNCLE MORRIS. I did. I was walking. But I came back. *(The men look at each other.)* I said I'd go, I was a big shot then. I'm sorry ... Judah Maccabeus I'm not. In those days, God used to talk to some people. Gave 'em visions. He'd whisper in their ears, on mountaintops, in caves, in deserts, especially deserts. He liked deserts; and they became like lions. But nobody speaks to me any more, only my landlord to raise the rent. Maybe I was having a vision before also, who knows? I'd go, but my bones are too brittle, one wind, one push, I'm in a convalescent hospital with tubes the rest of my life.. and with my luck, I'll have an anti-Semite for a nurse. *(Reaches the back door, turns back, with a waggish smile.)* Ai, to be seventy-five again and help out one of the widows. *(He exits. SEYMOUR tries lacing his boots.*

(JOYCE exits bedroom, clutching her keys, ready to go out.)

JOYCE. It's after one o'clock. They're not coming.

SEYMOUR. I'll meet them down there.

JOYCE. Please stop putting on those boots, Seymour.

SEYMOUR. Please don't ask me.

JOYCE. Don't get into a macho trip.

SEYMOUR. What macho? What the hell macho are you talking about?

JOYCE. Boots, fatigues. The guys together again. Parading around the streets clanging your machos together. I see it, Seymour, I see it.

SEYMOUR. You want to come? Come.

JOYCE. Why didn't you ask me *before?*

SEYMOUR. *Come on then.*

JOYCE. But how come you didn't ask me till the last minute?

SEYMOUR. Because I was afraid *you* might go, and I *wouldn't.*

JOYCE. I'm not trying for balls, Seymour.

SEYMOUR. *(He shoots up from couch, stalks around, the laces of his boots flapping.)* Whatever I draw salary, right to you; you spend it, you keep the checkbook, you pay the bills. Who made the decision to live in Beverly Hills? You did! West Hollywood where there's some *people* on the street, you said feh! a summer place in Malibu...

JOYCE. Trancas!

SEYMOUR. In *Malibu.* We can't afford Malibu. You said he bullish, fifteen percent interest, be bullish! Help with the dishes? Bullshit, it's me who does the dishes. It's you who doesn't help *me.* You're the mechanic, you even know what an exhaust manifold is on the car! And if you knew *where* it was, I think we'd be divorced already altogether. Where is this *macho* you're talking about? I marched on Hollywood Boulevard in the rain for the E. R. A., and *I* caught a cold and *you* didn't. *Macho?* I'll give you macho. I don't interrupt when you're talking; do I open the car door for you? *No!* I don't light your cigarettes, I cook most meals or we go to restaurants because you said *you* cooking was an antiquated act, and who orders the wine at restaurants? *You,* and you don't even drink! *What fucking macho?* And you know what? I don't even get on top of you lately because I didn't want to be accused of fucking in a reactionary position. And when you're on top of *me,* you get leg cramps! And we can never figure out how to do it from the *side* like other normal couples. Even with those sex manuals with diagrams! Wasted money!

JOYCE. Well, then speak up, goddamn it! I did!

SEYMOUR. All right!

JOYCE. Don't be the suffering martyr like your mother.

SEYMOUR. All right! I admire you for that.

JOYCE. Good!

SEYMOUR. But it's also a pain in the ass; I know, I hope we're going to come to something finally good, but *now*, any time you want your way, you don't argue it out, you try to intimidate me; hell! *Try?* You say everything's macho; macho this, macho that. Listen, is taking a piss standing up okay? I swear to God, I thought you were going to tell me taking a piss standing up was macho so now I sit down when I piss. I don't mind, I rest, but honest to God!

JOYCE. Are you accusing me of standing up to urinate?

SEYMOUR. When Keith was punched, you were almost glad he didn't fight back because it might be too macho.

JOYCE. I didn't say that. Can't we get out of here? We'll talk in the car. *(She crosses swiftly to the front door, opens it.)*

SEYMOUR. *(Races across stage and slams the door.)* You came close! Think about it!

JOYCE. I was shook up. I was rationalizing, okay. I was confused and furious and didn't know what the hell to do. Did you? You should have taught Keith to fight back.

SEYMOUR. How could I teach him to fight back when I never did?!

JOYCE. Then teach him to run away. He just stood there — you didn't know that, the teacher told me — the boy punched him and he stood there. It killed me. *Make him learn karate.*

SEYMOUR. You told me lay off. Don't give him a neurosis.

JOYCE. I was making excuses. You shouldn't have listened to me. I'm a *mother*.

SEYMOUR. I tried persuading him at the Dojo. He ..

(At that moment KEITH comes in. Whether he's been listening or not, we don't know.)

KEITH. I cried. You can say it. *(He crosses to the Intellivision, feigns playing machine.)*

SEYMOUR. So you cried.

JOYCE. You talk to him. You're his father. *(to KEITH)* And you talk to him too! *(With that she exits stage.)*

SEYMOUR. You didn't want to go to karate. *(KEITH shrugs.)* I won't force you to do something you don't want to.

KEITH. *(Nods enigmatically.)* I know.

SEYMOUR. Your face got bleak there, depressed. The more I talked about karate, the quieter you became. I felt terrible for you. My heart was tearing for you.

KEITH. I wasn't good at it.

SEYMOUR. Who's good at the beginning.

KEITH. Everybody was better than me.

SEYMOUR. They're doing it longer.

KEITH. Even those who started after me.

SEYMOUR. We all go at a different pace. Don't you learn things faster than other kids, then they catch up?

KEITH. You didn't like me then...

SEYMOUR. What? I .. no .. That's not...

KEITH. *(He doesn't want his father to lie.)* Dad...

SEYMOUR. *(anguished)* It was something else.

KEITH. You wanted another kind of son then ... *(SEYMOUR cannot lie, but he cannot tell the truth either. All that can come out is an anguished, strangled, half-moan, half-grunt.)* That's all right.

SEYMOUR. It's not all right. You don't be a nice guy!

KEITH. All right, Dad.

SEYMOUR. *Why must everybody love us?*

KEITH. *(Draws out something from his back pocket — a folded leaflet.)* Will they be there too?

SEYMOUR. *(Scans it quickly, looks up at KEITH.)* That-ball's-history...

KEITH. *(Shrugs his answer, takes the leaflet from his father. Points to boots.)* Do you have to go?

SEYMOUR. You don't want me to?

KEITH. I asked David and Scott. Their fathers aren't going.

SEYMOUR. What do you think?

KEITH. I'm just worried about you..

SEYMOUR. I'll .. I'll be okay.

KEITH. Really?

SEYMOUR. Really.

KEITH. But Mom said, in North Carolina...

SEYMOUR. *(Reacts by wiping sweat from his face.)* Yes .. I know..

KEITH. Then why, Dad?

SEYMOUR. I want those bastards to know I'm there.

KEITH. But they don't even know you.

SEYMOUR. Sometimes they have to know you.

KEITH. *(Nods as if he understands something deeply.)* If you take karate, I'll take it with you.

SEYMOUR. Don't do it for me. If you do it only for me, you'll quit.

KEITH. I want to take it.

SEYMOUR. You sure?

KEITH. Yes. Because I know you're not good at it either.

SEYMOUR. *(Doesn't know whether to laugh or cry.)* We'll go for a walk.

KEITH. Now?

SEYMOUR. No, no, I mean, sometimes, after, okay? *(KEITH nods, not fully comprehending, but he likes it.)* Now. Let me lace these, will you? *(He attempts getting the old frayed laces through the eyes, but is frustrated, wets the ends with spittle, his hands shake, tries again, fails.)* Damn. My hands.

KEITH. Here. *(The boy comes to SEYMOUR's side and quickly laces the boots for his father. SEYMOUR looks at his son for a second, then runs his hands through his son's hair. The boy doesn't look up, but suddenly hugs his father's leg. There's a moment.)*

SEYMOUR. *(Points to Intellivision.)* And don't let me win at that game either.

(JOYCE enters. She has a hard time controlling herself.)

SEYMOUR. *(His hands steadier now, finishes lacing one boot as KEITH finishes lacing the other. He stands up, moves around, tries the fit — grimaces.)* Oh, God, Joyce. You're right! My feet have grown. I can't walk.

JOYCE. They'll stretch. Walk around. And stop blaming me for your inadequacies. You piss any way you want. You had a lifetime before you met me. *(with humor)* And Three Mile Island? I did not cause Three Mile Island. The Medfly yes, but not Three Mile Island.

(JERRY enters, sees what's going on.)

JERRY. *(to JOYCE)* Stop him!
JOYCE. I can't stop him, he's not a baby.
SEYMOUR. *(Opens closet, tries to decide on jacket.)* I can't find a jacket.
JOYCE. *(Pulls one out.)* Here.
SEYMOUR. No, I mean a *hard* jacket. Something strong, thick. These all look so, *thin. (She finds a rugged hooded car coat; he throws it on hood and all, he turns around — he's pulled the cord to the hood, we can hardly see his face now. He heads toward door.)* Okay, I'll see you. *(He gets to door, opens it and steps out. Then almost as quickly, steps back in, closes door behind him, locks it, leans with his back against it.)* What am I doing? I don't have to do this. I don't want to do this. This is behind me. I'm a big business manager now; I have my own firm, you know how many people work for me? — I have big clients. People consult with me about the most complicated business matters. They listen to me. Nobody from Beverly Hills does this. I have giant debts. I never said anything about it, but I'm a little nauseous this morning. That's right. Look at my hands. They're sweating. My underwear is wet, I mean, I'm sweating between

my legs, dripping, boxer shorts. They said they were coming for me, and they didn't. Isn't that right?

JERRY. That's right!

SEYMOUR. I don't know where to go, what about orientation, who do you see? What do I do when I get there, or what about parking? There's no parking downtown. Nothing. We should go to K-Mart. I didn't even eat yet. So a few psychos wear swastikas, Nazism isn't native to America, it's totally foreign, gain a foothold here? Forget it, it's not homegrown, don't you see? No one pays attention to them anyway. If anything bad happened it wouldn't be Nazis again, it would be some high tech, computerized American version. This is for the police and government. I got plenty of other problems. I've got no time for this, and I'm studying karate with my son!

(Just then the doorbell rings loudly, impatiently.)

SEYMOUR. Oh, God.
JOYCE. What should we do?
SEYMOUR. I don't know.

(Another long insistent ring.)

SEYMOUR. They might break the door down.

(JOYCE breathes deeply, goes to door opens it. DOUG's enormous bulk fills the doorway; he shifts his weight and we see SUSANA behind him. They enter.)

DOUG. Come on, man, you got it together?

SEYMOUR. Together? Well .. not *all* together .. Some of it's together, some of it's not together.

DOUG. *(Points to tied car-coat hood that exposes barely a nose.)* Let's go. Take that off, you'll be blind on both sides. *(SEYMOUR sheepishly takes off hood. DOUG heads to door, turns, sees SEYMOUR is not following him.)* Well?

SEYMOUR. Listen, I've been thinking ..

DOUG. Once you're in the car, you'll be all right.

SEYMOUR. I'm scared, Doug.

DOUG. Listen. Do the thing you fear, and the death of fear is certain.

SEYMOUR. Uh, not necessarily. *(He starts untying a boot.)*

DOUG. I gotta go. I'm late. You coming, Seymour?

SEYMOUR. You're young; I have clients, I'm in business, uh, see, there's this guy Ralph Klein who's in competition with me, steals my clients ... Why were you so late? I could've been gone already. You know that? There could've been nobody here. That's right!

SUSANA. Oh, man, it's a waste. It's a cop-out. Come on, Doug.

JOYCE. He is *not* a cop-out!

DOUG. Is it a waste, Seymour?

SEYMOUR. Huh. You call me Seymour, it sounds like a real name. Not a joke.

DOUG. Seymour, I can't fuck with you now, they got a new wrinkle. They're writing books the Holocaust didn't happen, we made it up, a Jewish *hoax*. Does that frost your balls or don't it?

SEYMOUR. *WHAT?*

DOUG. Don't what me! All you guys are always *whating*

me, like you don't know this shit's always coming down, one way or another, you all ask *what?* You're shocked! Well, I'm shocked you guys are always shocked. Like you're virgins, you never saw a pussy before, you're living on Mars. You're no virgin, and this ain't Mars, so stop the shit. *(a bitter sandpaper bark)* "The Hoax of the Six Million." *Come on,* They're waiting on me.

SEYMOUR. Tell me now!

DOUG. We found out! We got 'em infiltrated. That's their speech at the Convention — that the Holocaust never happened. It's a myth created by Jews to collect reparations; you want to choke? — the death camps of The Third Reich are an invention of Zionist propaganda! They got maybe a hundred books and shit from all over, in seven languages yet, that deny it! They say it was the guilt of the Western Christian nations, about what happened to the Jews "supposedly" which caused them to vote Israel into existence and support Israel. But if the Holocaust didn't happen, then the birth is illegitimate. That's their new wrinkle. They're trying to illegitimatize Israel — and you know for what purpose!

SEYMOUR. *(truly shocked)* That's monstrous. I don't believe you!

DOUG. *(Slams book in SEYMOUR's hand.)* Here, pal. *(reads)* "Did Six Million Really Die?" Christian Vanguard, Crusade Church. P.O. Box 3247, Los Angeles, California. *(white hot)* So fuck you and the horse you rode in on, baby! Nazis and their friends say Jews who died were victims of wartime food shortages, concentration camp diseases, and the rest went illegally to America. The photographs of the dead? The newsreels? They were faked. Or Germans killed by Allied bombing. And get this, you really want to get crazy? This is part of their scam today. Herman Goering said he hadn't heard of The Extermination Camps until the Nuremberg Trials, and what he was told there didn't convince him! *(DOUG barks a terrible, bitter sandpaper laugh.)* It didn't convince *Herman Fucking Goering.* I love it. Next, us Americans'll be forced to prove there was a Pearl Harbor! *(He turns to the door, to SEYMOUR.)* They're waiting on us! Come on, Susana. *(DOUG waits for a reply, looks to SEYMOUR, doesn't get one. DOUG shrugs, SUSANA and he stride for the door, open it and head out.)*

SEYMOUR. *(Jumps up, shouts to his wife:)* All right, goddamnit! So I'm a Zionist Hoodlum! Fuck Vanessa Redgrave! *(Rushing, he joins DOUG at the door.)* Stay near me.

DOUG. I can't. Once you're down there, everybody's on their own.

SEYMOUR. Oh, God! *(He hesitates slightly, but only slightly as DOUG and SUSANA exit. He is almost out the door when:)*

JOYCE. Seymour! *(He stops in mid-motion. JOYCE rushes over, emotionally throws her arms around him and crushes him to her. He does the same, they clinch to each other. Then he is out the door.)*

(Immediate blackout. Dim area light comes on stage right illuminating shadows behind a scrim. Sounds are heard behind the scrim. The sounds grow louder. It's a crowd of two opposing forces,

AFTER CRYSTAL NIGHT

yelling, shouting, hoarse angry human noises. The lighting is dim, but now we can only see silhouettes of people of two opposing camps kept apart by uniformed police. Now we hear the crash of cymbals, drums and the harsh martial music of the Horst Wessel Song. *One side of the opposing forces screams in outrage. The other cheers. The music grows louder. A tasseled, tailor-made Nazi Standard creeps just over the scrim so that we now see the swastika. Suddenly, a harsh, violent voice shouts,* "Death to the Jews," "Finish Hitler's Work." *Suddenly, another Standard begins to peek out over the scrim, a rough cardboard drawing of the Star of David with a clenched fist embossed on it. Another voice flings back:* "Fuck you, Nazis." *The Nazi Standard shakes violently. Then disappears below the scrim. So does the "Never Again" Standard. The peace is broken. Violence breaks out — both groups surge into each other. The Police shouting orders, pandemonium as the fight rages. Total blackout. We are black a beat. Then the lights quickly come up. It is some hours later. The stage is empty. The TV set is on to the local 6:00 P.M. news.)*

TV ANNOUNCER. ...the State Senate voted overwhelmingly in favor of the measure and the Governor is expected to sign the Bill immediately ... In downtown Los Angeles a Jewish Defense League demonstration protesting a meeting of the American Nazi Party erupted into a brief club-swinging melee — *(JOYCE comes in from kitchen drawn by TV.)* that ended in the arrest of ten J.D.L. members.

JOYCE. Oi! *(Film of the fight goes on, and JOYCE watches, riveted, but as it gets rougher, she crunches up on the couch almost hiding her eyes with her forearm from the painful sight. She tries to take two or three different and contorted positions not to see the coverage but simply can't resist. Now she stands up and watches, biting her knuckles.)*

TV ANNOUNCER. The rally, held by fifty Nazi Party Members wearing uniforms, helmets, swastika armbands and carrying a red and white swastika flag, was held at the Republic Auditorium. *(She backs up as obviously the odious sight of the swastikaed Nazis are shown parading.)*

(KEITH has come down the stairs, carrying his tote bag, joins his mother, his eyes riveted on the T.V. He sets his tote bag down and we can now see K. GOLDSTEIN has been restored on the tote bag.)

TV ANNOUNCER. At least seven persons were injured — *(She pulls back from the TV set with a sharp intake of breath.)* — before the J.D.L. demonstration was declared an unlawful assembly and dispersed. *(Now she lets out a large sigh of relief.)* The violence started in front of the Republic shortly after two P.M., when a Nazi taunted a J.·D.L. picket with "Kill the Jews" and "Into the ovens, finish Hitler's job." An estimated fifteen J.D.L. demonstrators poured into an alley leading to the meeting hall and beat five men to the ground. *(More TV pictures flash on, and JOYCE now draws face-to-face with the TV set. KEITH joins her.)* After about forty police arrived on the scene, one of the beaten Nazis...

JOYCE. *(involuntarily)* Good!

TV ANNOUNCER. ...pointed out the J.D.L. members he said attacked him. About a dozen demonstrators then scuffled with police. *(Again her concern for her husband regis-*

ters in more body language, her almost closed fingers in front of her face, peeking out.) At least several persons suffered head injuries from police batons ... And now a commercial message... *(She punches the TV off and still with her hands clasped tightly to her face, prowls the room. Then she prowls it again. She turns the TV on again, but even before the picture or sound comes on she punches it off!)*

(The phone rings!)

JOYCE. *(Rushes to the phone.)* Hello! *(listens)* Jacob! Yes! I saw it on TV. Yes. TV. No! Don't say that. He did not faint! ... I don't know where he is!

(Suddenly the door bursts open and there's SEYMOUR, his carcoat torn, a blood-soaked hanky against his nose. He's bloody and bruised, but strangely, wildly jubilant and triumphant!

JOYCE. *Seymour! Are you hurt!?*
SEYMOUR. *(triumphant)* Yes! *(To speak he takes the hanky from his nose, a gush of blood streams out. She reacts.)*
JOYCE. *SEYMOUR!!* *(She buckles. But even though he catches sight of his blood he steadies his wife.)* Blood! You're hurt!
SEYMOUR. Yes! I'm hurt! — Look! *(He holds high a mud-stained, torn Nazi flag.)* *I got it!*
JOYCE. Seymour, are you all right?? You're hurt!
SEYMOUR. He was there, Joyce! *He was there!*
JOYCE. Who? *(Inspects his cut face.)* Your *nose,* your *eye...!* *(She tries to dab it with her hanky.)*
SEYMOUR. *(He brushes it aside.)* It's just blood. It'll be all right. I can't believe it, *he was there!*

JOYCE. What, Seymour, who was there!

SEYMOUR. *(a rising shout)* He was there. Mendl! He-was-there! *(Suddenly, he bursts in tears. Tears of passion, rage, exaltation, possessed by deep, powerful emotions.)* He was there! He was the screenwriter! He changed his name, but it was still Mendl. *(He is crying now.)* HE WAS THERE!!

JOYCE. Oh God, Seymour, Mendl!

SEYMOUR. He saw me just after the fight — and he cried. Joyce, Mendl cried when he saw me. I had this in my hand— *(He shakes his closed fist with the ripped Nazi flag.)* — and he cried when he saw me; you should've seen him, Joyce, he was the old Mendl, fighting two cops to get at the Nazis! He yelled, they were dragging him away... *(He can almost not go on.)* Do you know what he yelled? "Seymour, I still can't do Algebra!!"

(All stage lights have dimmed except for the small ring of brightness encircling SEYMOUR.)

SEYMOUR. He's in the hospital, he's hurt. But you can't kill Mendl! Never! Never! NEVER AGAIN!

(Slow fade to black as the curtain comes down slowly.)

THE END

PROPS

STAGE

ACT I, SC. 1
- Glasses on bar
- Seltzer bottle on bar
- Liquor, glasses on shelves behind bar
- Ashtrays (1 on bar, 1 on coffee table)
- Cigarettes in box on coffee table
- Napkins (on bar)
- 2 Joysticks for computer game (downstage with TV)
- Wastebasket (DL)
- Coat hanger in closet
- Telephone on bar

ACT I, SC. 2
- Glasses on bar
- Seltzer on bar
- Telephone on bar

ACT II
- Chinning bar (closet door)
- Sunday paper (coffee table)
- Telephone (on bar)

HAND

- Book (Joyce)
- Glass (Joyce)

Sandwich (Keith)
Tray with teacups, honey, lemon, teapot
Beer bottle (Joyce)
Nazi leaflet (Joe)
Briefcase (Mr. Cohen)
Jewish Bulletin (Mr. Cohen)
Papers (Mr. Cohen)
Glass of water for Cohen (Joyce)
Checkbooks (Seymour, Jerry)
Pens (Seymour, Jerry)
Cane (Uncle Morris)
Schnapps glass (Seymour for Uncle Morris)
Cigarettes (Joyce)
Lighter (Joyce)
Valium (Joyce)
Leaflet (Seymour)
Purse (Joyce)
Newspaper ad (Joyce)
Leaflet (Joyce)
Keys (Joyce)
Coffee cup (Jerry)
Sports bag (Keith)
Boots (Seymour)
Vacuum cleaner (Joyce)
Lemon Pledge (Seymour)
Duster (Seymour)
Booklet (Doug)
Checks (Uncle Morris)
Pen (Doug)
Nazi Banner (Seymour)
Bloody rag (Seymour)

COSTUMES

ACT I, SC. 1:
SEYMOUR — Suit, shirt, tie, oxfords, hat one size too big

JOYCE — Two-piece lounging outfit, expensive

KEITH — Jeans, t-shirt, sneakers

JERRY — Casual slacks, silk shirt, jacket, loafers

UNCLE MORRIS — Slacks, jacket, sweater vest, shirt, tie, hat, cane, scuffed shoes

JOE — Casual slacks, shirt, no tie, sneakers

DOUG — Jeans, t-shirt, denim jacket, boots

SUSANA — Fatigues, sweats

MR. COHEN — Stylish three-piece suit, power tie

ACT I, SC. 2
SEYMOUR — Pyjamas, slippers

JOYCE — Robe, slippers

ACT II
SEYMOUR — Wash pants, polo shirt, loafers

JOYCE — Sporty, morning outfit, expensive

KEITH — Jeans, t-shirt, sneakers

JERRY — Slacks, silk shirt, loafers

UNCLE MORRIS — Jacket, slacks, shirt, tie, hat, cane, scuffed shoes

DOUG — Similar to Act I with the addition of sturdy jacket

JOE — Similar to Act I with the addition of sturdy jacket

SUSANA — Similar to Act I with the addition of sturdy jacket

SEYMOUR — Duffle coat

PS 3569 .H3319 A7 1986

Shaner, John Herman.

After crystal night